Railways of Telford

DAVID CLARKE

THE CROWOOD PRESS

First published in 2016 by
The Crowood Press Ltd
Ramsbury, Marlborough
Wiltshire SN8 2HR

www.crowood.com

British Library Cataloguing-in-Publication Data
A catalogue record for this book is available from the British Library.

ISBN 978 1 78500 094 2

FRONTISPIECE: Black 5, 45237, pulls away from Wellington with a
Shrewsbury to Stafford stopping train on 21 April 1962. M. MENSING

Typeset by Servis Filmsetting Ltd, Stockport, Cheshire
Printed and bound in India by Replika Press Pvt. Ltd.

Contents

Acknowledgements

No author can write a book without the valuable assistance of others and I would like to mention the photographer Michael Mensing, who, despite living in Hampshire, took many photographs in the Telford area in the late 1950s and early 1960s and who sadly passed away in December 2014 aged 80. I for one remain in his debt.

The photographic content of the book is considerably enhanced by the inclusion of a number of the late Arthur Dodd's (A.J.B. Dodd) photographs. He lived in the Telford area until 1960, but returned to the area many times afterwards as his family lived in St Georges. Arthur's in-laws' next door neighbour was a signal man at Hollinswood signal box, so Arthur had access to the yard area, providing excellent photographic opportunities. Arthur died in 1974, but his son Mike is the proud custodian of his father's collection and has spent many hours sorting through it, scanning the negatives and answering queries from me. The only problem with Arthur's photographs is that he did not record the date, time or place. Between Mike and myself we have managed to find most of the locations, although the dates are more problematic.

The librarian at the Ironbridge Museum Trust, Joanne Smith, was very helpful on my visits to the museum's archives. My thanks also go to Geoff Cryer for his help and for the use of some of his photographs and to R.A. Cooke for using some of the drawings from his excellent book on the track diagrams of East Shropshire. Tom Heayside supplied some excellent photos, and Bob Yate helped with details of the Lilleshall Company. Thanks also to my friend Martin Neild for proofreading the book and eliminating my poor grammar.

Lastly, many thanks to my wife Glenis, who has put up with me spending a lot of time writing this book.

Introduction

As a resident of Trench (near Wellington) during my teenage years in the 1960s, I became familiar with the railways of the area that would subsequently be redeveloped as Telford New Town. Initially, I would cycle to Trench Crossing station and take the train either to Shrewsbury via Wellington, or to Stafford to go trainspotting. In 1962 and 1963, I used to travel by train from Wellington to Wolverhampton to visit my grandmother every two weeks. In 1965 and 1966 (as the line through Trench Crossing had lost its passenger services in 1964), I used to cycle to Wellington to travel further afield using a British Railways rail-rover ticket. Also being interested as a teenager in industrial archaeology, I visited the area covered in old mines, slag heaps and other derelict industrial buildings. As a pupil at what was then Trench Secondary Modern (now renamed The John Hunt School) along with a school friend (Richard Softley), we undertook to photograph some of the derelict sites for a school project. This involved tramping through the woods and industrial dereliction of the area. Unfortunately, the photographs we took have subsequently disappeared, so cannot be used in this book. For one of the summer holidays I worked at Russell's Rubber Company adjacent to Trench Lock and the long-abandoned Trench Inclined Plane and had my very first taste of beer in 'The Shropshire Arms' public house, which was on the opposite side of the canal basin from the works.

Therefore the writing of this book is a labour of love for me, not only because of nostalgia, but also to produce a book that documents the railways of the area. A number of excellent books have been written on individual lines (*see* the Bibliography at the back of the book), but as far as I'm aware this is the first attempt to produce a book covering the whole area and should act as a 'taster' for further in-depth reading. The research for Hollinswood Yard threw up lots of information and this part of Telford has not been covered before. The building of Telford New Town in the late 1960s has radically changed the landscape, with much of the industrial past swept away and open fields covered in new industrial estates. Industrial dereliction was nothing new, with large parts of the area covered in old spoil tips and long-abandoned buildings, and this was one of the reasons the area was considered ripe for development and the building of the new town.

I have tried to concentrate on the operation of the railways in the Telford area and have therefore simplified the somewhat complex arrangements of the various railway companies that would eventually be swallowed up by the London and North Western Railway (LNWR) and Great Western Railway (GWR) companies.

In 1963, the first staff to be appointed for the creation of what at that time was called Dawley New Town moved into Hartfield House near Horsehay to start the planning for what would eventually be renamed Telford New Town, with the job of transforming 200 years' worth of industrial dereliction and its associated spoil heaps. The complete restructuring of the area commenced to the point that most parts are now completely unrecognizable from how they were in the 1950s. The area now known as Telford can be seen on the accompanying maps.

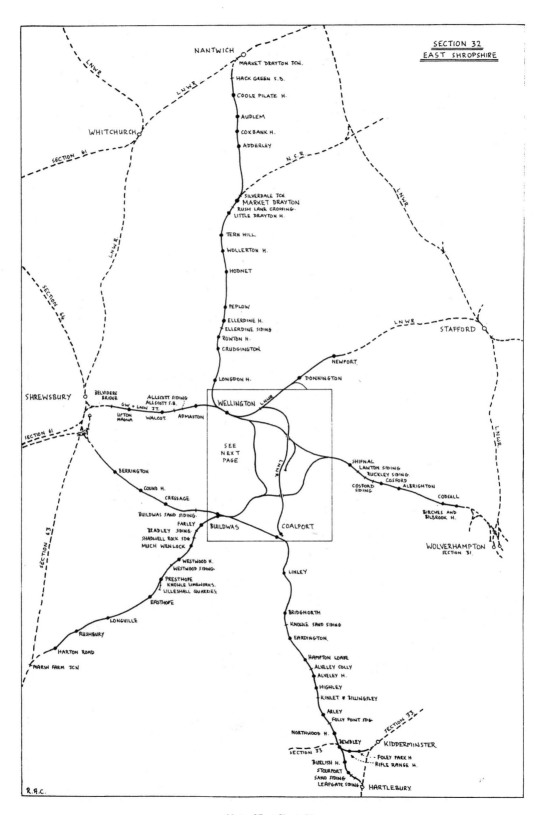

Map of East Shropshire.

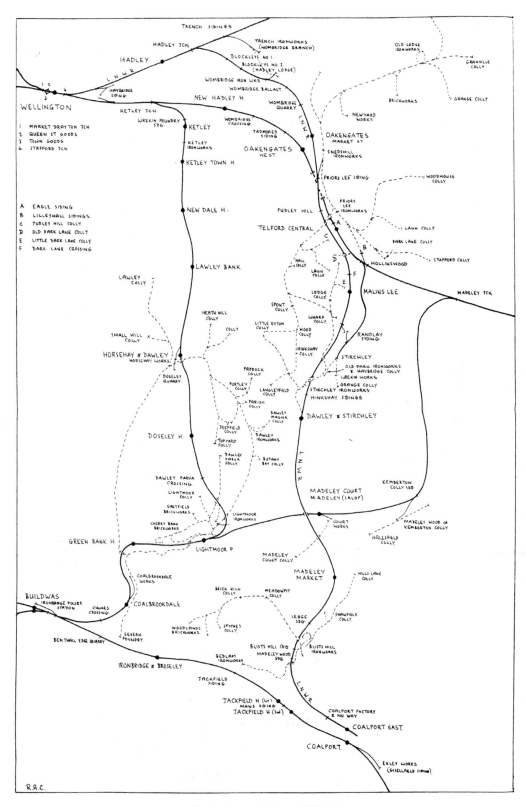

Detailed map of the area of Telford.

CHAPTER I

The Industrial Revolution in East Shropshire

The Area Before the Industrial Revolution

Before one can consider the railways in the Telford area we need to look at why the area required such an extensive railway system. East Shropshire had extensive coal reserves and outcrops of coal were known to have been worked by the Romans at Oakengates. Coal mining continued through the Middle Ages. The mines of this period were relatively small, with the shafts only being about 60–100ft (20–30m) deep, and this type of mining continued into the twentieth century. An unfortunate consequence of this was that subsidence became a chronic feature of the area. Many of these small pits were not documented and many had quite short working lives. The mining for coal also revealed deposits of ironstone and fireclay, enabling iron smelting to be undertaken. A blast furnace was known to have been opened in Lilleshall village in 1591.

The Industrial Revolution in Shropshire

There is some debate amongst historians regarding the period of time that should be considered as the Industrial Revolution. The consensus view is that the date range is from around 1760 to 1830, which was then followed by a second Industrial Revolution between 1870 and 1890. The Industrial Revolution can be considered one of the major turning points in human history, impacting on every aspect of life. It was characterized by an increase in average incomes and economic growth. The area known as Telford was to play a major part in this world-changing process.

One of the key elements of the Industrial Revolution was the transition from using charcoal to coal for the production of iron and steel, which resulted in the cost of producing iron being significantly reduced. For a given amount of heat, coal required much less labour to mine than cutting wood and converting it to charcoal, plus coal was available in much greater quantities.

The use of coal for smelting iron actually started in 1678 with the reverberatory, or air furnace, but this was an inefficient process and was not widely adopted. In 1708, Abraham Darby at his furnaces at Coalbrookdale developed a technique using coke to fuel his blast furnaces, which enabled him to reduce the cost of producing pig iron. By the mid-1780s, Abraham Darby II was building new furnaces at Horsehay and Ketley, such that coke pig iron was now cheaper than charcoal pig iron and could for the first time be considered a structural material. This was given a huge boost by the building of the Iron Bridge over the River Severn by Abraham Darby III in 1778.

The supply of cheaper iron and steel impacted on other industries, such as nail-making, chain-making, hinges, wire and other hardware items, as well as to the growing machinery and engine industries. One quarter of the iron produced in Britain in 1806 came from East Shropshire.

The Coalbrookdale Company built blast furnaces at Donnington Wood in 1783. The discovery of fireclay also enabled brickworks to be opened where tiles, white bricks, firebricks and land drainage pipes would be made. The brickworks at Wrockwardine Wood and Donnington Wood were originally based at small mines where fireclay was produced as a by-product of coal mining before the brickworks was expanded in 1793.

Such was the passion for cast iron that John Wilkinson, an ironmaster, promoted the use of iron for all sorts of products, including kerb edges, and he developed the small iron boats (known as tub boats) that were used in the canals and which could be pulled up the inclined planes. Parallel with the improved quality of the iron produced he invented the first precision boring tool for the manufacture of cannon for the navy.

The great iron steamship, the SS *Great Britain*, built in 1843 by Isambard Kingdom Brunel, was constructed of wrought iron plates supplied from the Coalbrookdale area of Shropshire, with the plates arriving at Bristol by barge on the River Severn. It is thought that some of the workmen employed on building the SS *Great Britain* came from the Shropshire ironworking district, as they had experience of making small canal boats in iron and the riveting techniques required.

One of the key features of the Shropshire ironmasters was the existence of companies combining ironworking with mineral extraction and then integrating this with the ironworks, including blast furnaces, forges and rolling mills, as well as in some cases foundries and engineering shops.

The Coming of the Railways

With the growth of mining, brick-, tile- and iron-making and the production of many iron products, the big problem was getting the raw materials into the various works and then the finished products away to market. Originally, the location of Abraham Darby's works in Coalbrookdale was a combination of local supplies of wood for charcoal and local iron-stone, then subsequently local supplies of coal. The adjacent River Severn enabled the finished goods to be taken downriver to Worcester, Gloucester and Bristol and upstream to Shrewsbury. However, the river was not the most reliable of transport systems, with inconsistent water depth causing problems during the summer months, leading to reductions in the loads carried by the boats. One other unusual disruptive factor reported in 1734 was the appearance of a British warship at Bristol Docks, which resulted in many of the bargemen and crews of the river boats avoiding the area because of fear of being 'press-ganged' into the Navy! In 1756, over 100,000 tons of coal was shipped from the collieries in Broseley and Madeley.

Whilst the River Severn provided the only means of transporting coal and goods out of the area, there was also the problem of getting raw materials into the ironworks (and also moving coal from the mines into the river boats). The only means of achieving this was by teams of packhorses. The solution to this problem was twofold – the development of canals and the creation of tramways, which consisted of wooden rails laid down on a roadway and the coal and iron carried along them in 50cwt wagons with iron wheels.

Several canals were built in the area and these incorporated a number of inclined planes to cater for the hilly countryside. The first canal was the Donnington Wood Canal, which opened in June 1767 and served the Lilleshall Company. Other canals followed in 1788, 1797 and finally in 1832. There were five tunnels and seven inclined planes linking the canals together, highlighting the difficulty of building canals in a hilly area. To get the raw materials to the canals, a system of tramways soon developed and these gradually got longer and longer, with one of the tramways being 8 miles (13km) in length. Some of the difficulties with the canals in the heavily mined areas were subsidence causing leakage from the canals and the inclined planes being expensive to operate.

The first recorded use of a wooden railway in the area was in 1605, when a line was built from

Jackfield down to the River Severn for moving coal from the mines down to the ships on the river. Abraham Darby II built such a tramway in the 1750s based on the plateways used in the north-east of England, but with many improvements such as the use of cast wheels and iron axles.

Soon the area became covered in these early tramways transporting not only coal, ironstone and limestone, but also clay and fireclay into the tile- and brickworks. The tramways were further developed in 1767 when the Coalbrookdale Company produced the first cast-iron rails for the plateways and by 1785 there were over 20 miles (32km) of iron plateways. The use of iron rails was a considerable improvement over wooden rails, as they were less likely to wear out or collapse and also enabled larger wagons to be used. The motive power for these tramways was horses for the longer distances and manpower for short distances, although oxen

were used on road wagons and it is assumed they may also have been used on the plateways. The limit now on the plateways was the use of horses to pull the trains of wagons. Abraham Darby also made the obvious move by opening new furnaces at Horsehay and Ketley (in 1755), which had coal mines immediately adjacent to the ironworks, reducing the amount that needed to be transported by the plateways.

The area was soon covered in plateways and even after the coming of the canals and the standard-gauge railways, plateways continued in use for many years, with the last horse-drawn plateway between Lightmoor Brick and Tileworks and the foundry at Coalbrookdale, which did not close until October 1932.

The coal-mining bonanza in East Shropshire led to a blitzed landscape and it has been estimated that over 6,000 mine shafts were sunk in the East

Before the proper railways appeared, the Coalbrookdale area was covered in plateways pulled by horses. Here some of the surviving plateway wagons and track are seen near the Coalbrookdale Company works.

Shropshire coalfield. Coal production peaked in Shropshire in 1871, when 1 million tons were produced. From that date onwards, production gradually declined. As an example of the decline of coal mining, the Lilleshall Company had fifteen coal mines in 1891, but this had reduced to five mines in 1915 and by 1947 had further reduced to two.

The twentieth century is a story of decline and finally the ending of underground mining in this coalfield. Many pits closed through exhaustion of reserves, but economics also played its part. A combination of the great depression, losses incurred during miners' strikes (particularly the 1921 and 1926 strikes), manpower shortages and increased competition from the Staffordshire Coalfields led to a series of pit closures. Ironstone production ceased completely in the early part of the twentieth century, but clay mining remained active in the southern part of the coalfield. The last fireclay mine, The Rock, which actually lies in the northern part of the coalfield, closed in 1964.

At Nationalization of the coal industry, there were three principal deep mines remaining open – Granville and Grange Collieries of the Lilleshall Company and Kemberton Colliery of the Madeley Wood Company. A few small private pits also operated. Most of the small mines were soon closed, but small private drift mining did not finish until Shortwoods Mine, near Wellington, closed in 1971. Under reconstruction, Granville and Grange Collieries merged into a single unit in 1952. After this date, the Grange shafts were used solely for ventilation purposes. Kemberton Colliery finally closed in 1967 through exhaustion and, with the closure of Granville Colliery in 1979 through heavy faulting, underground coal mining ended in Shropshire.

Similarly, the production of iron from furnaces peaked in the middle of the nineteenth century. In 1862, there were seven different companies owning thirty-two blast furnaces in the area, but this had fallen to fourteen furnaces by 1878, producing 100,000 tons of pig iron – about half of what had been produced in 1868. The reality for the railway

companies was that soon after they had arrived in East Shropshire many of the industries they served were in slow decline, although these industries would still generate profitable traffic for them until the 1950s.

What is also clear from looking at the competing railway lines in the area was how the local companies took advantage of the fierce competition between the railway companies, with many sites being served by two rival companies, so the Lilleshall Company had access to the LNWR from the Coalport branch and also at Donnington, as well as the Great Western at Hollinswood. Randlay Brickworks had access via the LNWR Coalport branch at one side of its works and from the Great Western at the other (Stirchley or Old Park branch), so could decide which carrier to use based on price and service. A similar situation occurred at Haybridge Iron Company, which had sidings on both the LNWR and GW lines.

The coming of the standard gauge main-line railways to East Shropshire was dependent upon the opening of railways elsewhere. In 1837, The Grand Junction Railway (GJR) linked Birmingham (via Wolverhampton) and Stafford to Liverpool and Manchester. In 1848, the Shrewsbury and Chester opened the line between those two locations, so the railways were getting closer, but needed further construction to take place.

The Shrewsbury and Birmingham Railway and the Shropshire Union Railway and Canal Company (usually abbreviated to Shropshire Union or SU) had been given authorization to proceed with their plans, so the two companies shared the construction of the railway between Shrewsbury and Wellington. They also shared the operation of the lines. The railway opened from Shrewsbury as far as Wellington in June 1849, with the route to Wolverhampton being opened in November 1849.

In parallel to this, the Shropshire Union was constructing the line from Stafford to Wellington, which also opened in June 1849, but the company was now leased to the LNWR. This period was one of consolidation and the Shrewsbury and

Birmingham became part of the Great Western Railway in September 1854.

In 1867, the line from Crewe via Market Drayton opened with a junction on the Shrewsbury side of the goods yard, which was controlled by Wellington no.4 signal box. The line was absorbed by the Great Western in 1877, giving the GWR a through route to Crewe and Manchester.

So by the 1870s, East Shropshire was connected to the wider national rail network and had direct links to the Black Country and London, as well as Crewe and Shrewsbury. The branch lines to Coalport and Buildwas meant that the heavily industrialized region now known as Telford was well served and raw materials could be brought in and finished goods flow out.

0-6-2 tank 5690 is seen at Wellington no.4 signal box in July 1959 with a northbound freight. Diverging to the right is the line to Market Drayton and Crewe, with the main line to Shrewsbury straight ahead. M. MENSING

CHAPTER 2

Wellington and the Main Line

Wellington

As the principal station of the area and certainly the busiest, it seems appropriate to start our journey around the railways of Telford at Wellington. There are still a number of trains working through the station, despite the closure of several of the lines that once fed into the station. From an architectural point of view, it is very much the same station that emerged from the rebuilding in 1888.

Wellington is the largest town in the district and has a long history. It was given the right to hold a

One of the distinctive features of Wellington station was the brick water tower that had one corner cut away to allow trains to pass from the island platform and is seen here in 1960. Note also the ex-LNWR water crane on the platform. R.G. NELSON

A view of Wellington from the footbridge looking towards Shrewsbury in August 1960 with Wellington no.3 signal box in the distance. The two goods yards were just beyond the road bridge. R.G. NELSON

market in the town in 1244 and continues to be a market town to this day. As such, much of its wealth has derived from agriculture, with a large cattle market and a potato market, as well as maltings and breweries (there were two in the town, Wrekin Ales and Shropshire Breweries). The industries in the town were also agricultural-based, with foundries catering for agricultural equipment. There was also a church and school furniture manufacturer, plus a large wood yard and sawmill. The town was large enough to have its own gasworks converting coal into town gas.

The station is in a cutting with road bridges crossing the railway at either end and is dominated by All Saints Parish Church, which originated in mediaeval times. This church provides a significant landmark when trying to identify photographs with no description on the back. The original photo-

graph of a Webb 2-2-2-2 three-cylinder compound clearly shows the church in the background.

Given its location and the fact that it was a junction station with routes to Stafford, Crewe, Shrewsbury, Wolverhampton and branches to Much Wenlock and Coalport, the station was a sizeable affair, although the station entrance was very modest, almost hidden away down a sloping carriageway from the main street of the town. Up until the mid-1960s, the station was very busy particularly on a summer Saturday when numerous holiday trains would pass through non-stop.

As the line from Stafford Junction (Wellington no.1) at Wellington through to Shrewsbury was joint with the LNWR and GWR, agreements had to be made as to which company was responsible for the infrastructure and signalling. When the line through Wellington was built, the

Wellington station was accessed by a modest entrance sandwiched between the platforms and the shops in the centre of Wellington and this is clearly shown in July 1962 with a Royal Mail van backed up to the gate giving access to the platform. PATRICK KINGSTON

signalling infrastructure was purchased from independent signalling companies. The Shrewsbury and Birkenhead Joint Railway was administered by a Joint Committee and in the 1860s through to the 1880s both the parent companies were busy with work on their own lines and left the Joint company staff pretty much on their own. Signalling work was put out to tender, the company with the lowest quote winning the business. In 1880, approval was given for the enlargement, rebuilding and resignalling of Wellington station and this included extending the main-line platforms and building the covered over-bridge for passengers, as previously passengers crossed by a boarded walkway – not ideal on a main line!

The four new signal cabins were of a new design, with an overhanging roof of a distinctive Saxby and Farmer style. From January 1885, the LNWR became responsible for all signalling matters on the joint line and from that point on, as renewals and alterations were made, the characteristic LNWR signal and signal arms appeared. For maintenance purposes, the Shrewsbury and Wellington line was absorbed into the LNWR Stafford district, which meant that the Stafford District Engineers Inspection Saloon pulled by a Webb 2-4-0, *Engineer Stafford*, would be seen at Wellington. In LNWR days, the District Engineers' saloon was pulled by a dedicated locomotive complete with nameplate.

In 1904, the District Engineer responsible for engineering work moved from Stafford district to Bescot (near Walsall) and *Engineer Walsall* would have been seen with the Divisional Engineers' Inspection Saloon. The use of a dedicated locomotive for the inspection saloons ceased during London, Midland and Scottish (LMS) days, with the

Stafford Junction with Jubilee 45579 Punjab from Burton shed approaching Wellington from Stafford with a Shrewsbury-bound train in the early 1960s, passing Wellington no. 1 signal box. Burton Jubilees were a common sight on the Stafford line after moving to the shed from various top link depots. RAIL-ONLINE

One of the Lilleshall Company's own-built locomotives, 0-6-0 no.6, is seen here c. 1900 with one of the company's wagons. IRONBRIDGE GORGE MUSEUM TRUST

Wellington no.3 signal box, erected in 1908, remained in use until 1969. D. CLARKE

ex-LMS 4-4-0s and Ivatt Class 2 2-6-0s, to diesels of Class 24, 25, 47. In diesel days, it was whatever was to hand, which resulted in a Warship diesel, D809 *Champion*, on one occasion.

In 1903, the maintenance arrangements were revised and the GWR took over responsibility for the Shrewsbury district lines including Wellington, but a further change in 1909 meant that Wellington was again the responsibility of the LNWR. Wellington no.3 signal box (at the end of the platform facing Shrewsbury) was extended in 1913.

Wellington was controlled by four signal boxes. No. 1 (twenty-two levers and closed in September 1967) was opposite the line in from Stafford and was known as Stafford Junction. It controlled the line to Stafford and Coalport. No.2 signal box (seventy-two levers) was located in the station opposite the end of the two bay platforms and controlled these platforms and the eastern end of the Crewe platform loop. The box was renamed Wellington on 30 September 1972 when the box replaced all the other

saloon being pulled by any available locomotive. This continued into British Rail (BR) days, with the LMS Inspection Saloon being seen at various times with different locomotives pulling it, ranging from

The LNWR was responsible for signalling and infrastructure at Wellington and the district civil engineer for the LNWR was based at Stafford, so the Engineers' Inspection Saloon and dedicated locomotive Engineer Stafford would have been seen on the line. D. CLARKE

The early signal boxes at Wellington were provided by the signal company Saxby and Farmer, but in 1952 Wellington no.2 was replaced by a BR version in brick and before the replacement box was commissioned both boxes could be seen side by side. Note the grand Victorian gas lamp on the platform. D. CLARKE

Wellington signal boxes. No.3 signal box (fifty-eight levers and closed in September 1967) was at the end of the platform facing Shrewsbury and controlled the roads into the engine shed, the west end of the Crewe loop platform and access to both the Queen Street and Town goods yards. Wellington no.3 was replaced by a brick and concrete signal box in 1952 and it was intended that this would replace the other three signal boxes, although this was not achieved until the early 1970s.

No.4 signal box (forty-six levers and closed in September 1973) was known as Market Drayton Junction and was located adjacent to the junction

for the line to Crewe. It controlled the western ends of the two yards, as well as the Market Drayton and Crewe branch.

Wellington no.3 finally replaced all the other signal boxes at the station in September 1973. The box was renamed 'Wellington' and had fifty-eight levers. The use of numbers for the four signal boxes was a hangover from the LNWR, as this is how that company would differentiate signal boxes in the same location; the GWR way would have been to call the boxes 'Wellington South' or some other name to differentiate them, rather than use a number.

The most notable change to the track layout in the 1980s was the complete removal of the track from the far side of the bay platform and the removal of all signs of the locomotive depot, which has now become a car park. D. CLARKE

Given that Wellington was a joint line, the goods facilities were split between the two companies, with the LNWR having the goods yard on one side of the line (the up) called Queen Street Goods, and the GWR having a goods yard on the opposite side (the down), known as Town Goods. The GWR had connections from its yard into a wood yard and sawmill owned by R. Groom and Sons, but from the 1940s very little timber was being delivered to them, with the bulk now arriving by road. There was also a connection into the Wellington Gas Company gasworks. The gasworks sidings were on the GW side, but the coal for the gasworks came via the LMS from north Staffordshire, so in theory the wagons should have been shunted by the LMS shunter, the ex-Caledonian 0-4-0, but the fourteen wagon loads were beyond its capability. However, only the little 0-4-0 tank was low enough and light enough to enter the works, so the GW shunter (usually a pannier tank) would propel the loaded wagons into

the works with twelve empty wagons. These were used as barrier wagons, enabling the loaded wagons to enter the gasworks, but not the locomotive. In the 1950s, the sidings into the works were extended, allowing twenty wagons at a time to be delivered.

The GW yard performed two functions, the sorting and marshalling of trains and also the delivery of loads to the various merchants that had premises in the yard, including John Gough, Coal Merchants, who were established around 1905 and were the only coal merchant on the GW yard. They received wagons of coal from Granville, Littleton (Cannock) and Kemberton, with anthracite coming from Mountain Ash in South Wales. When the business was at its height, up to six wagons a day were being delivered. Shell also had an unloading facility in the yard and received petrol tankers from Ellesmere Port and Avonmouth.

Although the LMS had a cattle siding adjacent to the cattle market, there was also a cattle dock on

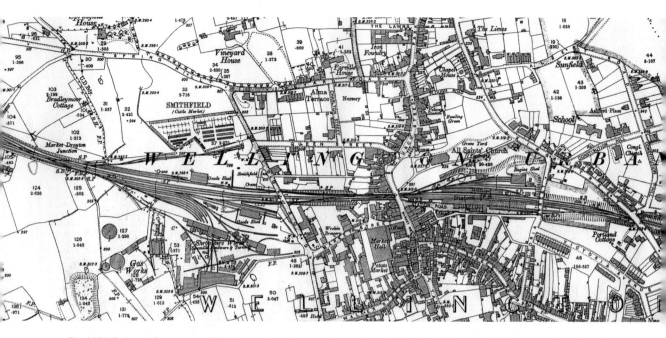

The 1901 Ordnance Survey map of Wellington shows the extensive goods yard of the Great Western, which had more sidings than the LNWR on the opposite side, with the GW yard also servicing a wood yard.

the GW side. Wagons for the outbound traffic would have to be ordered in and would depart as a special train. The bulk of the cattle traffic was outbound, with very little coming in, cattle generally arriving at the Monday cattle market by lorry. Animal feeds also arrived in sacks and were delivered for three companies. The sacks would be stored in the GWR warehouse before being delivered by railway lorries.

View looking towards Wolverhampton taken in 1982, with the ex-LNWR yard on the left and the ex-GW yard on the right. D. CLARKE

View of the ex-GWR goods shed at Town Goods, Wellington, in 1982. D. CLARKE

The GWR had nine marshalling sidings, with some used for specific locations, so siding 1 was used for the Craven Arms line, Ketley, Horsehay, Coalbrookdale and Buildwas. Siding 2 was used for local stations Wellington to Wolverhampton (Oakengates, Hollinswood, Shifnal and so on). Siding 3 was used for Shrewsbury traffic, with sidings 4, 5 and 6 used for any destination. Siding 7 was used for South Wales traffic, which in practice meant the 12.40am goods to Shrewsbury Coleham. Siding 8 was used for wagons that would be transferred at Shrewsbury and siding 9 was used for any destination.

Sometimes the loads on the local trains and the use of pannier tanks meant that, for instance, the 3.10pm freight for Horsehay would be banked out of the yard all the way to Ketley station, usually with another pannier tank, but sometimes with a 44XX 2-6-2 tank; the bankers were spare engines and not one of the yard shunters. After

reaching Ketley, the engine would return light to Wellington.

Space was at a premium in the GW yard, particularly if some empty cattle wagons had been delivered and the 7.05am Crewe to Hollinswood freight would be in the yard from 11.18am to 1.45pm. The amount of shunting at Wellington Town Goods was huge, with shunting taking place 22 hours per day, giving a total of 132 hours per week. The author suspects that this level of shunting activity was dictated by the relatively cramped siding accommodation, which had no space in which to keep the wagons. It is also probable that the creation of Hollinswood Yard in the 1920s enabled the GWR to move some of its sorting from Wellington to Hollinswood.

The LMS goods yard known as Queen Street Goods had fewer sidings than the GW yard and was shunted by the Trench Sidings' shunter. As this shunter would leave at 10.15am, the author would

View of the ex-GWR yard Town Goods taken in the 1980s facing towards Shrewsbury. The yard to the right is the ex-LNWR Queens Street.
D. CLARKE

assume that any further shunting would be performed by train engines bringing freight into the yard.

Like the GW yard, there were a number of merchants receiving traffic, with five separate coal merchants operating from the yard: Shropshire Associated Collieries; Harry Maiden; Robert Williams; Arthur Mason; and Stockley and Tudor. Deliveries were made by a mixture of lorries and horses, the last horse for coal delivery taking place in the mid-1950s. Similarly, the LMS still used horses for delivery well into BR days, again finishing in the 1950s. As an example of the dedication to their work, one of the carters in the yard, Bill Hicks, would walk 7 miles (11km) to the yard from Madeley, as if he caught the bus he would arrive ten minutes late. He continued this until he retired at seventy. Coal came from the following collieries, Granville, Littleton (Cannock) and Kemberton, with Harry Maiden receiving six wagons a week.

Potato merchants J.E. England and Sons also operated out of the yard, from their own warehouse. McGowan and Sons ran a fruit and vegetable business, again with their own warehouse, which included six heated ripening rooms. Esso had a petrol depot on the LMS side, with tank wagons arriving from Ellesmere Port and Avonmouth.

The cattle market was located just behind the LNWR Queen Street Goods and a rail connection to a cattle dock was provided, but by the 1930s much of the outbound cattle traffic left via the GWR. If there were cattle wagons on the LMS side with a load, these would be sent out on a regular freight, not a special train as per the GW side.

Before the grouping, the two companies would have to trip work wagons between the two yards and sometimes the LMS shunter used part of the GWR yard to give some room for shunting on the LMS side. With Nationalization in 1948, the distinction between the two yards became less important.

Black Five 45392 is seen at the freight yards at Wellington in July 1965. The sidings to the left are the former LNWR Queens Street Yard and on the right the former GWR Town Goods. Both were still reasonably busy, but the railways were losing freight at an alarming rate, so they would soon disappear. M. PAIGE

Wellington goods yards during the 1960s seemed to have been used for the sorting of coal trains to and from Granville to Buildwas and retained the use of a Class 08 shunter. The yard also had allocated to it an ex-GWR shunter's wagon, no.41802, marked 'Wellington (Salop)'. With the closure of Wellington no.4 signal box in 1973, a ground frame was provided on the up side and one on the down side.

As with all goods facilities after the 1960s, the yards were gradually reduced in capacity, with all of the Queen Street Yard being removed in June 1982 and the bulk of the down side by 1982. The down ground frame was taken out of use at the same time.

The LNWR influence on Wellington station was still visible in the early 1960s, with an LNWR water crane still at the south end of the main line platform facing Wolverhampton. Subsequently, the main line through Wellington from Wolverhampton to Shrewsbury came under the Western Region, whilst the line to Stafford remained the responsibility of the LM Region. In September 1963, with further boundary changes, Wellington again was passed to the LM Region.

A general view of Wellington station in 1960 looking towards Shrewsbury. A Much Wenlock train sits in the bay platform with 9741 at its head.
R.G. NELSON

The Main Line through Wellington

The growth of freight traffic after the line opened meant that the joint goods depot was soon operating at capacity and a Shropshire Union goods depot was opened at Wellington in 1854.

The GWR commenced running fast trains from Shrewsbury to London in 1855, but passengers had to change trains at Birmingham as the line onwards was broad gauge. However, from 1866, following the conversion to standard gauge, through trains enabled passengers to remain onboard without having to change from one gauge to the other.

The station now catered for trains to and from Crewe via Market Drayton, Wellington to Coalport, Shrewsbury to Stafford services and Wellington to Much Wenlock and Craven Arms.

Wellington Station

The station, having been enlarged and rebuilt in 1881, had five platform faces, two of these on the main line and two through tracks, enabling trains to pass through the station. Adjacent to the locomotive depot was an island platform, with one platform facing the main line. This platform was used by the expresses from the Shrewsbury direction and the Shrewsbury to Stafford trains. The other side of this platform facing the locomotive depot was generally used for the Market Drayton and Crewe trains.

The main-line platform face was bidirectional, as sometimes a parcels train for Crewe or Shrewsbury would be facing the wrong way. The island platform lost the line facing the locomotive shed in 1969 when the trackwork in the locomotive depot yard was removed because the Crewe trains had ceased in 1963. The opposite main-line platform was used again for the expresses from the Wolverhampton direction and for the Stafford to Shrewsbury trains.

The two bay platforms were principally used by the Much Wenlock trains and the service to Coalport. Some of the Stafford Shrewsbury trains would also use one of the bay platforms. One of these platforms was removed in 1969. The remaining bay platform, despite the cessation of the Coalport services in 1952 and the Much Wenlock trains in 1963, stayed in use for parcels traffic and later for permanent way vehicles, and remains so to this day.

The track layout at Wellington remained pretty much the same until well into the 1980s, with the major change being the simplification of the trackwork into the bay platform. Here we see the layout looking towards Wolverhampton in 1982. Just past the signal box can be seen the retaining wall for the original signal box replaced in 1952. D. CLARKE

The two bay platforms had an unusual method for releasing the locomotives and getting them to the other end of the train without the need to foul the main line. There was a line set on a gradient, up which the loco could push the train out of no.3 bay

(usually only two coaches) to a stop block. Then a shunter would put on the handbrake in the guard's van, release the vacuum and uncouple the engine and let the coaches run back into bay platform no.4 by gravity. The locomotive could then reverse in on

In the early 1980s, the bay platform had been reduced to one line and is here seen being used for storing a track maintenance train pulled by a Class 08 diesel shunter. By 1985, the track in the bay platform had been completely removed and the bay filled in. D. CLARKE

Fairburn tank 42186 is seen at Wellington with a train to Stafford. No shed plate is visible, but Stafford received this engine in June 1962 and had a small number of these tanks for the Shrewsbury trains. The railcar in the background had arrived from Much Wenlock on the last day of the Wellington to Wenlock services.
M. MENSING

to the front of the train. A small wooden hut opposite the signal box was provided for the shunter and can be seen on many photos of Wellington. This spur siding was taken out of use and removed in September 1961.

After leaving Wellington heading towards Wolverhampton, the line to Stafford is passed to the left and immediately on the left was the Haybridge Iron Company nestling in the V of the Great Western main line and the LNWR Stafford line. Sidings serviced the ironworks and its successors until 1969 and up until 1932 were controlled by a signal box that was normally switched out. When a train was due to call at the sidings (the 3.05pm from Wellington running on Mondays, Wednesdays and Fridays), the box would need opening. This was done by the signal man at Ketley, who would have to walk from Ketley to the signal box at Haybridge, where he would open the box and carry out the signalling and point changes required by the train. Upon the completion of the shunting, the signal

man would hitch a ride back to Ketley in the brake van, as the freight would be heading for Ketley and Horsehay. In his absence, the Ketley Station Master would perform the duties of signal man.

In 1932, the signal box was replaced by a ground frame with three levers. As with many ground frames, it was locked, in this case by Wellington no.1 signal box. The signal man there would unlock the ground frame from his signal box to allow the guard of the train to carry out shunting. As with many other sites in the area, the Haybridge Ironworks also had sidings from the LNWR line to Stafford.

As the train heads towards Wolverhampton, Ketley Junction was passed on the right. This was used by trains for Coalbrookdale, Buildwas and Much Wenlock. The junction also had a couple of sidings and was controlled by a signal box that opened in 1911 and was closed in September 1967.

Having passed Ketley Junction and climbing up a gradient, New Hadley Halt was reached.

View from a diesel railcar of New Hadley Halt, which was on the main line between Wellington and Oakengates; the simple wooden platforms can be seen. D. CLARKE

New Hadley Halt

This was opened in 1934 by the GWR to try to beat off competition from buses. The platforms were simple wooden ones with no buildings. The station was closed in 1985 just before the new Telford Central station was opened.

After passing New Hadley Halt, Wombridge Crossing was reached.

Wombridge Crossing

This was not a station, but a small signal box that protected a road crossing. The signal box was more like a covered ground frame. The crossing was closed to vehicles on 16 October 1966 as part of the New Town development and the signal box was closed on the same date.

A 0-6-2 tank approaches Wombridge Crossing, which was located between Oakengates and New Hadley Halt and had a signal box to control the crossing gates. The road crossing was taken out of use in 1966. A.J.B. DODD

Padmore's Sidings

After passing Wombridge Crossing on the right, there used to be set of sidings initially known as Padmore's Sidings, but some of these had been removed by 1883. However, Maddox & Company then used these remaining sidings until 1902.

Shortly after passing Padmore's Sidings and before the station was reached, there was a signal box on the left, then Oakengates station was reached.

Oakengates Station (GWR)

Oakengates was a substantial station with sidings on both the up and down side and two separate goods sheds. One of the sidings carried on to serve Millington's wood yard. This was also served by the LNWR Coalport branch, which at this point was only a few hundred yards away from the GW station. The yard and the block section were controlled by a signal box, which was open until September 1967.

Oakengates GWR on the line to Wolverhampton and its goods shed facing Wellington is seen on 7 July 1963. P.J. GARLAND

Oakengates GWR in July 1963 looking towards Wellington and showing the signal box and small goods yard. P.J. GARLAND

Oakengates GWR looking towards Wolverhampton with Oakengates tunnel in the distance. R.G. NELSON

Oakengates in July 1963 facing towards Wellington. P.J. GARLAND

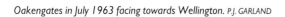

Oakengates station in 2013. G. CRYER

The station also had an overbridge, a necessary item given that the station was on the very busy Great Western main line.

The crossover and sidings were taken out of use in January 1965, but in 1968 two sidings and a ground frame for Tunnel Cement (later Castle Cement) were installed. The cement sidings were installed to provide cement for the huge building programme that was needed for Telford New Town. These sidings had been taken out of use by April 1994 and removed, but the connection remained.

After leaving Oakengates, the line passes through Oakengates Tunnel with its ornate brick-work entrances. The tunnel had been originally constructed to broad gauge, but before the lines were installed it became standard gauge. As with many tunnels, the portals at each end were of different design.

Having left the tunnel, the line passed the large Lilleshall Priors Lee site on the left before reaching the extensive sidings at Hollinswood.

Hollinswood Yard

With the building of the Lilleshall Company works at Priors Lee, the company needed an interchange with the adjacent Great Western main line and Hollinswood Yard was constructed in the 1870s. The yard was extended and upgraded a number of times. The original signal box was closed in 1883 and replaced by a signal box on the Wolverhampton side of the junction with the Stirchley branch; this was closed in 1911.

The GW main yard was created in 1929 and by the 1950s had fourteen sidings with buffer stops, as well as two sidings with points at each end. There were also five long head shunts, three on the down side and two on the up side. The long head shunt on the up side is regularly seen on photographs showing trains heading for Wolverhampton. The Stirchley branch had three dead end sidings parallel with the main line and one longer dead end siding parallel with the branch.

8F 2-8-0 48478 works past Hollinswood with a freight on 27 August 1962 towards Wolverhampton. In the background can be seen the head shunt sidings that interchanged with Hollinswood Yard and the Lilleshall Company at the rear of the train. M. MENSING

The final signal box on the site was opened in 1911 and extended in 1928. It was close to the site of the first signal box.

The yard had three main components. The first was a set of sidings specifically for the traffic in and out of the Lilleshall Company, with two dead-end sidings and six sidings coming to a point at the single-line connection into the Lilleshall Company's own railway system. In addition, the Great Western yard was used as a concentration point for wagon loads from around East Shropshire, which were sorted before being sent onwards. Third, there

4-6-0 7828 Odney Manor passes through Hollinswood Yard from Wolverhampton heading for Wellington. The freight-only Stirchley branch runs off to the right. The yard sidings are to the immediate left, with the former interchange yard with the Lilleshall Company visible behind with the coal wagons. A.J.B. DODD

was a set of sidings to sort wagons for the Stirchley branch.

As well as sidings for the sorting of wagons, Hollinswood had two up loops (travelling towards Wolverhampton), with accommodation for forty-eight wagons, and one down loop, with accommodation for fifty-eight wagons, which would allow a slower freight to be pulled in whilst a faster train could pass. The loops were also provided with water cranes for locomotives to replenish their water tanks.

Outgoing traffic from the Lilleshall Company was pig iron, bricks, concrete products and tiles, as well as coal. Incoming traffic consisted of coke, limestone (from the Lilleshall Company's own quarries), as well as iron ore from Spain, Sierra Leone and low-grade ore from the Banbury area. The limestone workings from the company's quarries were trip-worked into Hollinswood Yard from Wellington.

A service from Presthope (on the line between Much Wenlock and Craven Arms) also ran to Hollinswood, presumably with limestone that was quarried at Presthope and would be used at the Priors Lee furnaces of the Lilleshall Company.

In 1909, the *LNWR Working Time Table* noted that a joint ballast train would be run into Hollinswood Yard.

The *GWR Working Time Table* for 1936/7 has shunting at Hollinswood being carried out in three shifts, with some of the shunters being provided by Wellington shed and some by engines arriving at the yard, for example the second shift utilized the engine from the 11.05pm from Oxley. One of the Oxley to Shrewsbury freights would have a second engine at the front and this would be detached at Hollinswood for shunting, minimizing light-engine working. In 1937, the *GWR Working Time Table* listed shunting for fifty-four hours per week, including three hours on Sundays. However, this had risen to 150 hours per week by 1947.

The Great Western built a small number of shunting trucks and one of the last batches built in 1947, no.41834, was allocated to Hollinswood in 1954 and in 1961. These shunting trucks enabled the shunters to move around large yards safely without the need to hang off the side of engines. The shunting trucks also carried spare shunting poles, sprags, spare lamps and anything else the shunters might need during a shift. A similar shunting truck, no.41802, was allocated to Wellington and was branded 'Wellington (Salop)'.

A number of goods trains from Oxley to Croes Newydd and Oxley to Crewe would arrive at Hollinswood, but not depart for some considerable time, so the assumption is that wagons were detached and added in the yard. So, for example, the Oxley to Crewe goods would arrive at 4.24pm, but not depart until 5.40pm. Certainly a Tysley fireman

4-6-0 7818 Granville Manor *and a 2-6-0 pass through Hollinswood Yard with a summer extra heading towards Wolverhampton. In the background the chimneys of the Lilleshall Company Priors Lee works can be seen and the sidings on the far right are for Lilleshall Company traffic.* A.J.B. DODD

stated that Hollinswood had freights leaving for Kingswinford, Stourbridge and Worcester, fed by local services but also by the numerous Crewe trains. In December 1940, a Castle Class 4-6-0 was seen on a Croes Newydd to Hollinswood freight with forty-three wagons and in 1948 a 28XX no.3848 was also observed on a Croes Newydd to Hollinswood freight with forty wagons.

During the 1930s and until the early 1960s, Oxley shed had some 2-8-2 tanks allocated (7213, 7217, 7218, 7238 and 7247 being allocated in late 1959 and 1960) and these would be used on the Oxley to Crewe freights, as well as working an Oxley to Hollinswood freight, and would then work a Hollinswood to Stourbridge Junction freight. One of Oxley's 2-8-2 tanks, no.7226, was unusually pressed into passenger service in July 1947 when observed at Wellington.

Other freight services originating at Hollinswood were to Shrewsbury, Wellington and Buildwas. The Crewe broccoli train would also stand at Hollinswood from its arrival at 1.40pm until its departure at 2.00pm. It is not clear whether vans were detached from this train.

There were also regular engine and van workings between Wellington and Hollinswood.

Hollinswood Yard was not only used for the interchange of traffic in and out of the Lilleshall Company's works, but also as sorting sidings for coal traffic from Granville Colliery on its way to Buildwas Power Station. It also dealt with coal from Kemberton Colliery, as well as freight from the Stirchley branch. When Buildwas Power Station opened in 1932, a number of Midlands collieries also supplied coal for Buildwas as well as Granville and these wagons would be sorted at Hollinswood. With the closure of the Lilleshall system in 1958, the coal traffic from Granville Colliery could not get to Hollinswood Yard via the Lilleshall internal railway system, so the trains went down the line from Granville to Donnington, from there to Wellington and then to Madeley Junction and Buildwas.

Empty coal wagons were also delivered from Buildwas to Hollinswood for sorting before being made up into trains for Granville Colliery. Because the coal trains from Granville to Buildwas had to reverse at Wellington and at Madeley Junction, the trains required brake vans at both ends. One of the jobs therefore for the 'Hollinswood Shunt' loco from Wellington was to take a number of brake vans up to Hollinswood.

In 1952, there was a Shrewsbury (Coleham) to Hollinswood Yard goods departing at 3.45pm and returning to Shrewsbury Coleham at 7.15pm from Hollinswood. Ex-GW 2-6-2 tank 4118 was

An empty coal train with 43026 of Crewe South shed at its head from Buildwas is seen near Oakengates on 1 October 1964 heading towards Wellington, where it would reverse and go down the Stafford line to the interchange sidings for Granville Colliery. *RAIL-ONLINE*

seen on this service at Shrewsbury. The Stirchley branch closed in 1959 and the sidings opposite to Hollinswood were removed in 1962.

In later years, the amount of coal trains sorted at Hollinswood decreased and by 1969 most of the sidings had been taken out of use, leaving just a loop and a couple of sidings. These were closed in 1972, followed by the signal box at the end of July 1972. By then, the Granville to Buildwas coal trains were using air discharge hoppers and brake vans were no longer required. In 1986, the new Telford Central station was opened just to the west of Hollinswood Yard.

The Hollinswood shunt was the preserve of Wellington shed, but with its closure in August 1964, Oxley shed at Wolverhampton provided the motive power, with BR Standard Class 2-6-0 no.76022 being observed in October 1964. The traffic into the yard was further reduced in 1967 with the closure of Kemberton Colliery.

With the decline in the use of Hollinswood Yard in the early 1960s, it also acted as intermediate storage for condemned locomotives being towed to various scrapyards in the West Midlands from all over the country and also for the storage of wagons on their way for disposal. The stored wagons would

be worked in and out of the yard as special trains. In the 1960s, the disposal of steam locomotives was beyond the capacity of the British Railways workshops to scrap them, so a policy of selling locomotives to private scrap merchants commenced. The problem here was that each locomotive was sold to the highest bidder, not necessarily the nearest scrapyard to where the locomotive was residing after withdrawal.

Towing withdrawn steam locomotives over long distances was a real nuisance for the operating department, as the speed of the convoy (usually two or three locomotives at a time) was restricted and each locomotive in the group being towed would require someone on the footplate unless a guard's van was used. These convoys of engines would travel from place to place, where they would be parked until another crew and a clear path could be found for them. It was also not unknown for these small convoys to be pulled by one of the condemned locomotives, but, if not, other towing locomotives would need to be found. Locomotives going on the ex-GW main line through Wellington to Wolverhampton would generally be towed to a number of scrapyards in the West Midlands (particularly Cashmore's at Tipton) and would usually have another stopover at Oxley shed in Wolverhampton, where they could be parked before moving on for the last stage of their one-way trip to oblivion.

The Stirchley Branch and Associated Industries

This branch was a freight-only line of 1.5 miles (2.4km) and was formally known as the Old Park branch. The branch had no signal box and was operated by one engine in steam, with the train crew holding a token to give them possession of the line.

The line curved away from the Great Western main line at Hollinswood opposite Hollinswood Yard and served Randlay Brickworks and the large complex that was Old Park Ironworks, as well as Grange Colliery. The branch was initially worked by the Haybridge Iron Company. On the Ordnance Survey plan for 1902 it is described as a mineral line, and by then the Grange Colliery was closed and disused. From 1908, the Great Western Railway took over the maintenance and workings of the branch.

The Old Park Ironworks became Wellington Iron and Coal Company in 1872. By 1902, the ironworks no longer operated and the site was taken over by the Wrekin Chemical works, which manufactured Naptha and tar from timber with the wood residue converted into charcoal. The chemical works closed in 1932. In 1901, the extensive furnace slag mounds from the old furnaces led to the creation of a slagworkss; here the slag was crushed and then coated with tar and bitumen. A concrete works was also set up, again using the slag as a raw material. The slag heaps were depleted by 1941 and both plants closed. As well as the standard-gauge trackwork, there was a network of tramways connecting the Chemical works and Stirchley Ironworks that crossed over the Coalport branch.

The Stirchley branch was closely shadowed by the LNWR branch to Coalport, with the LNWR line also sending in a spur to the opposite side of the Randlay Brickworks. Further down the branch, the LNWR also had access into Old Park Ironworks and

Hinkshay pits. The close proximity of the LNWR and GWR lines showed the ferocious competition between the companies to access the various works in the area.

The working of the branch was the responsibility of a Wellington shunter, the loco running light-engine to Hollinswood before proceeding down the branch. The *GWR Working Time Table* for 1936/7 only shows one train with the instruction runs as required, with the train calling at Randlay Brickworks, Tarslag works, Wrekin Chemicals and Bilston Slagworks. If the train ran, it would only call at any of the works if required. Any wagon loads would be taken back to Hollinswood Yard for sorting and then moving on.

What is also clear is the continual opening of mines and ironworks, but then closure became a constant theme, with works just being abandoned and left derelict for many years. Randlay Brickworks continued to operate until closure in 1964.

The branch closed on 2 February 1959, prompted by bricks no longer being sent out by rail from Randlay Brickworks. The track was removed shortly afterwards. The sidings specifically for the Stirchley branch had been removed by November 1962.

Leaving Hollinswood Yard, the next feature on the line would be Madeley Junction.

Madeley Junction

The junction was located on the line between Wellington and Wolverhampton and allowed coal from various collieries (including Kemberton) to be sent out, as well as for coal trains for Buildwas Power Station from Granville Colliery to be worked down to the power station. The layout of the junction allowed trains from the Wellington direction to reverse at the junction so that the train could work forward to the power station, as the trains had brake vans at both ends. A refuge loop for the main line was also located at the junction and had capacity for thirty-one wagons. The length of the loop at the junction restricted the length of the coal trains to 20–21 of the standard 16-ton mineral wagons

Madeley Junction in 1965 on the main line between Wellington and Wolverhampton (facing towards Wellington) provided a route into the coalfields of East Shropshire and is still in use today for the coal trains to Buildwas Power Station. KIDDERMINSTER RAILWAY MUSEUM

and many photographs show these relatively short trains. The normal procedure was for the train arriving from the Wellington direction to push the train through the junction and down the branch, then pull forward into the loop. The loco could then run round and couple up to what had previously been the back of the train, then proceed down the line to Buildwas. The GWR signal box was relocated in 1925, with the box moving nearer the junction.

Kemberton Colliery was also on the line between Madeley Junction and Lightmoor and coal from the colliery could be worked out via Madeley Junction, as well as through Lightmoor Junction.

In 1954 and 1955, some further changes were made to the layout and in 1969 the whole junction

Madeley Junction on 25 August 1962, with Castle no.5031 Totnes Castle *heading towards Wolverhampton with an express. The line to Buildwas can be seen curving away on the left.*
KIDDERMINSTER RAILWAY MUSEUM

Madeley Junction was remodelled in 1969. The original signal box was demolished and a new box built. The remodelled junction is shown here on 31 May 1970. D. CLARKE

was again remodelled. The 1925 signal box was demolished and a new signal box built in the 'V' between the branch and the main line. The new signal box had forty levers, replacing the thirty-four levers in the old signal box. The remodelling also moved the run-round loop away from the main line and parallel with the branch line, as the coal trains from Stoke would still have to reverse. By this time, brake vans were no longer required as end of train lamps were used.

The section of line controlled by Madeley Junction signal box was changed in 2002 and again in 2006, when Lightmoor Junction signal box was closed and Madeley Junction took over responsibility. The signal box at Madeley Junction was closed in November 2012 and demolished shortly afterwards. Control of the junction passed to West Midlands Signalling Centre at Saltley (Birmingham).

Operating the Line

This section will detail much of the traffic through the station, but also the traffic relating to the Stafford to Wellington line would by definition run through Wellington station. The passenger trains to and from Wellington to Crewe were modest – usually just two coaches. In the 1920s and 1930s, the trains were hauled by a motley collection of elderly Great Western locomotives.

During World War II, more unusual locomotives were seen through Wellington when Oxley shed received an allocation of London and North Eastern Railway (LNER) O4 2-8-0s during the 1940–3 period. In early 1943, twenty-five of the American 2-8-0s were also allocated to Oxley, but when they left in 1944, they were replaced by LMS 8F 2-8-0s until 1947, when these in turn were replaced by WD 2-8-0s. The LNER 2-8-0s made a short-lived comeback in 1951, when a small number of O4 2-8-0s were allocated to Oxley, but they only lasted a few months and all had been transferred away by September 1951 and replaced by WD 2-8-0s.

After World War II, the passenger trains for the Crewe line settled down to Pannier 0-6-0 tank engines supplemented by the Ivatt Class 2 2-6-2 tanks. For a short period in the 1950s, a small number of BR Class 3 2-6-2 tanks were allocated to

The variety of GWR locomotives used on the Wellington to Crewe line was extensive and here 3208, a Dukedog, is seen at Crewe waiting to depart to Wellington in the late 1930s. *HMRS*

Ex-LNWR 4-6-2 tank 6993 pauses at Wellington on 3 August 1935 with a Shrewsbury to Stafford train. *R. CARPENTER*

One of Stafford's Fowler tanks 42389 is seen at Wellington on 22 August 1957 with a Stafford train. The locomotive was a long-standing resident of Stafford shed. *D. CLARKE*

For the last few years of the Wellington to Crewe service, the Pannier tanks were supplemented by a small number of Ivatt 2-6-2 tanks and in June 1962 41204 is seen leaving Wellington with a Crewe service. 2-8-0 2866 is visible on the right. M. MENSING

Wellington (nos 82004, 82006, 82009 and so on) and as well as working the Much Wenlock trains, they were used on the Crewe trains.

The Crewe line also generated a substantial amount of freight traffic, usually hauled by most of the ex-GWR 4-6-0s, but in later years more ex-LMS locomotives such as Black Fives and 8F 2-8-0s. In the late 1930s, the value to the GWR of the line to Crewe via Market Drayton showed with a regular Oxley to Crewe service, as well as other services such as a Worcester to Crewe goods (via Wolverhampton) and a Crewe to Worcester empty vegetable, fruit and passenger coaching stock train. There was also a Crewe to Stourbridge Junction coal empties, plus a Kidderminster to Crewe goods service and a Worcester to Manchester goods via Oxley.

Oxley, on the outskirts of Wolverhampton, had a large marshalling yard and generated a significant number of freight services that would pass through Wellington with regular goods services from Oxley to Croes Newydd (Wrexham), as well as Chester to Oxley.

Some of the express goods services from Oxley via Wellington included a Birkenhead service, as well as a Bordesley Junction (Birmingham) to Birkenhead service. Similarly, there was a Birkenhead to Paddington express goods, plus a Birkenhead to Birmingham fast goods. Some of these long-distance fast goods trains to and from Birkenhead ran at night and were the preserve of the large-wheeled ex-GWR 2-8-0 47XX locomotives. Their use on overnight trains gave them the nickname 'night owls'.

The massive ex-GW 2-8-2 tanks were not a common sight at Wellington, but Oxley shed at Wolverhampton acquired four in the late 1950s. Here, 7247 of Oxley is seen at Wellington shed on 7 July 1956, presumably having worked a freight in from Wolverhampton.
R. BLENCOWE

In the 1930s, a number of the express goods passing through Wellington were of LMS origin, as follows: Camden to Shrewsbury, via Stafford; and Burton to Shrewsbury (probably a beer train). These express goods were classified in the *Working Time Table* as 'E' head code to differentiate them from other goods trains classified 'F', as through goods for the joint line. Amongst these 'F' head code trains were a Rugby to Shrewsbury service via Stafford and a Stafford to Swansea (LMS). The LMS would also run a coal empties from Shrewsbury to Donnington via Wellington. As well as the usual freight and passenger services from the Stafford line, there was a Wellington to Trench Sidings trip working in the late 1930s.

Up until 1931, the 2.10pm Paddington to Birkenhead train would 'slip' a coach for Wellington, avoiding the need to stop the train at the station. The coach would be detached from the speeding train by the guard in the carriage at Ketley Junction and, if judged correctly, would roll into Wellington station and be brought to a stand adjacent to Wellington no.2 signal box. The station pilot would then pick up the coach and bring it into the platform. If the guard misjudged the speed of the train, or was too enthusiastic with the brake and the coach stopped short, the signal box would give instructions for the station pilot to proceed 'wrong line' to collect the coach. Once the passengers had decamped, the coach would be taken to the

GW Hall 5933 at Wellington on 14 May 1951 with a rake of Southern coaches en route to Birkenhead from the south coast. The coaches were on alternate weeks Southern Region or Western Region. The point work for releasing coaches and locomotives from the bay platform can be seen on the right. E.R. MORTON

Town Yard. It would stay there overnight, to then be attached to the rear of the 11.02pm train from Wellington to Paddington. After 1932, the 2.10pm service stopped at Wellington, thus avoiding the slip-coach working.

In the 1920s, there was another unusual working. The 9.40am Bournemouth to Birkenhead train (via Oxford and Wolverhampton), arriving at Wellington at 2.50pm, would detach the last three coaches and these would then be sent to Crewe and onwards to Manchester, with the train from Wellington only stopping at Market Drayton. This was a fast train by Wellington shed's standards and was worked by GWR Barnum Class 2-4-0s and then GWR Bulldog 4-4-0s.

There were a number of longer distance services originating at Wellington, with a Wellington to Birkenhead train in the 1960s, which was seen at Shrewsbury with a Castle Class at the head. Presumably this had run light-engine to Wellington to work the service.

In the 1950s and 1960s, there were regular InterCity expresses from Birkenhead to Paddington, usually hauled by Castle 4-6-0s with six or seven coaches, but occasionally Hall Class 4-6-0s were in charge. In addition, there were Shrewsbury to Wolverhampton stopping trains, usually hauled by Shrewsbury's Counties, Halls or Granges, and there were also Wellington to Shrewsbury stoppers. The Much Wenlock and Crewe stopping trains were

The Birkenhead to Paddington expresses up until September 1962 were usually in the hands of Castle 4-6-0s and here 5026 Criccieth Castle *is seen on 7 July 1962 just before the service was handed over to the new Western diesels.* PATRICK KINGSTON

also still running, as was the Shrewsbury to Stafford and return stopping trains.

Freight services were also extensive, with many Birmingham to Birkenhead and Crewe services. A loaded iron ore hopper train was photographed and this was presumed to be heading for Wrexham and then to Brymbo Steelworks.

In the summer, a huge number of extra holiday trains were run. These did not stop at Wellington and were hauled by whatever motive was at hand at the sheds in the Birmingham area (usually Tyseley). Elderly ex-GWR 2-6-0s, sometimes double-headed, were often pressed into service with heavy loads. This practice continued into the 1960s and sometimes the only available motive power was not up to the job, for example on one occasion a BR Standard Class 4 2-6-0 had to stop a number of times on its way to Wellington to provide an opportunity to build up steam.

The Cambrian Coast Express was the best known of these services and was usually hauled by a London-based (Old Oak Common) Castle, from the London direction, but from 1951, following bridge upgrading, the ex-GWR Kings were allowed north of Wolverhampton and were sometimes seen on the train. Unfortunately, their use on these trains did not last long, as with the introduction of the Western Class diesels they were all withdrawn in late 1962. From then on, the Cambrian Coast Express would be hauled initially by the Westerns and later by the Class 47 diesels that had replaced the Westerns from 1964.

An exceptional working for the Cambrian Coast Express was BR Standard Class 8 4-6-2 no.71000 *Duke of Gloucester*, which was seen on the train to Wolverhampton on 19 December 1962 and returned through Wellington on a parcels train. In February 1961, Shrewsbury shed had some difficulty providing motive power for the Cambrian coast and so Stanier Black Five no.45283 was used extensively for the month.

The Wellington to Crewe passenger services stopped on 7 September 1963, although freight

An ex-GW 2-6-0 6342 is pressed into express passenger service in July 1962 with an extra northbound holiday train, probably for the Welsh coast, and heads for Shrewsbury without stopping at Wellington. PATRICK KINGSTON

The down Cambrian Coast Express with a Castle passes Madeley Junction in the snow. A.J.B. DODD

Ex-GW 2-8-0 2889 joins the main line at Wellington from the Market Drayton line, pulling a freight from Crewe in the 1950s. G. COLTAS

Castle Class 5019 Treago Castle pauses at Wellington on 6 October 1962 with a Birkenhead to Paddington train. At this time, the expresses were being handed over to the Western Class diesels and steam on these Paddington trains would soon become a thing of the past. G. SHARPE

A Black Five 45436 of Warrington (8B) shed departs from Wellington, having arrived from Wolverhampton in 1965, with the author having just left the train. The use of Black Fives on passenger trains marked the change to the LM Region. D. CLARKE

remained. By 1966, freight traffic on the Crewe line was still heavy, with seventeen down and up to twenty to twenty-two up workings along the line each day. The freight traffic was high as electrification was causing some disruption on the West Coast main line, so some freight services were re-routed. There still remained a single pick-up freight on the line, leaving Crewe at 7.15am and arriving at Wellington at 10.28am. It left Wellington at 11.40am and returned to Crewe. The line to Crewe was closed completely on 8 May 1967; the track remained, but had been removed by 1970. The last loco to work the line was Class 24 diesel no.D5002, which was seen with a train of redundant rails.

Some of the Shrewsbury to Stafford trains in both directions, rather than use the main-line platform, would go into one of the two bay platforms, freeing up the main-line platform for fast trains. The train would then either reverse out (if it was a Stafford to Shrewsbury train), or pull out on to the main line to continue its journey. On 29 August 1964, the passenger services between Shrewsbury, Wellington and Stafford ceased.

The express services between Birkenhead and Paddington were turned over to diesels at the start of the winter timetable on 10 September 1962, with the new Western diesels being introduced. Steam was used for part of the route, with the diesels monopolizing the Shrewsbury to Paddington section. If a Western was not available, a Warship would be substituted, with no.D815 *Druid*, D817 *Foxhound*, D828 *Magnificent*, D834 *Pathfinder*, D859 *Vanquisher* and D870 *Zulu* all being noted on these trains.

The Westerns (and occasional Warship) were replaced by the Brush Type 4 (Class 47) locomotives from January 1964 onwards. However, due to some problems with the Class 47s in late 1965 and early 1966, the Westerns reappeared. The last sighting of a Western on these services was D1066 *Western Prefect* in the summer of 1966.

Special trains were not usual in the area, except for the Talyllyn Railway Specials from Paddington

A number of special trains ran through Wellington over the years and here Stanier 2-6-4 tank 42482 is seen on a Stephenson Loco Society special in May 1958. This class of engine was not a common visitor to Wellington, as Stafford had the Fowler and Fairburn varieties. D. LAWRENCE

For the autumn timetable in 1962, the Birkenhead to Paddington services were handed over to the new Western Class diesel hydraulics and here D1003 Western Pioneer is seen on a southbound service in April 1963. RAIL-ONLINE

When the Paddington to Birkenhead services were dieselized in 1962, the primary motive power was the Westerns, but occasionally a Warship would be substituted and D817 Foxhound is seen passing Stafford Junction approaching Wellington on 27 August 1962. M. MENSING

One of Shrewsbury's Jubilees, 45577 Bengal, heads a train at Wellington that originated at Shrewsbury and is headed to Stafford. Shrewsbury's Jubilees and Standard Class 5 4-6-0s were regulars on the stopping trains between Stafford and Shrewsbury. RAIL-ONLINE

to the Cambrian coast and in the 1960s the preserved A3 Pacific *Flying Scotsman*. However, the 1960s saw an increase in enthusiast specials, with motive power not normally seen in the area, as on 10 February 1963 when a special train from Marylebone to Crewe passed through Wellington hauled by unrebuilt Southern Region Bulleid Pacific no.34094 *Mortehoe*. The train was run in freezing temperatures and snow and became progressively late, much to the discomfort of the passengers. Another example, Duchess Pacific no.46245 *City of London*, was seen on an Ian Allen special in 1964.

On 24 June 1966, a Merchant Navy Pacific, no.35026 *Lamport and Holt Line*, worked through Wellington with a Warwickshire Railway Society special from Waterloo to Crewe. The occasional

troop train could also bring unusual motive power, with BR Standard Class 6 Pacific no.72006 *Clan Mackenzie* being seen in the 1950s.

With changes to regional boundaries, more of the Wellington area became part of the LM Region and the motive power at places like Oxley (Wolverhampton) took on a distinct LMS look. Black Fives were seen on the trains from Wolverhampton to Shrewsbury and more of the freight was seen behind Black Fives and 8Fs.

Through services between Birkenhead and Paddington ceased at the end of February 1967. However, for six months in 1967–8, a Shrewsbury to London Euston via Wolverhampton High Level train was diagrammed for Warship haulage and D837 *Ramillies*, D843 *Sharpshooter*, D845 *Sprightly*,

D848 *Sultan*, D853 *Thruster* and D855 *Triumph* were seen on this service.

A rare sighting of Hymek Class diesels occurred in late 1970, when for two weeks a South Wales to West Midlands oil train was diverted through Shrewsbury and then on to Wolverhampton via Wellington with 7058, 7061, 7077, 7093 being observed on the train.

During the summer there was also a weekdays-only Bournemouth West to Birkenhead (Woodside) train, with its alternating set of green Southern Region coaches and Midland Region maroon stock. This train was usually hauled by one of Oxford's Hall Class 4-6-0s.

From 10 September 1962 for a period, the Pines Express (Manchester to Bournemouth and return) was run from Crewe to Wellington via Market Drayton and on to Wolverhampton. The motive power was usually an English Electric Class 4 (Class 40), but after the Market Drayton line was closed to passengers in September 1963, the train was re-routed from Crewe to Shrewsbury and the motive power became more variable, with Britannia 4-6-2s (such as no.70044 *Earl Haig*) and in May and June 1963 one of Edge Hill's rebuilt Scots, no.46110 *Grenadier Guardsman*, was noted every week. Western hydraulics also worked the train for a short time, so D1007 *Western Talisman* was seen in 1962 and D1035 *Western Yeoman* was seen early in 1963.

A relief to the Pines was also run in both directions and on 23 August 1963, Carlisle-rebuilt Scot no.46166 *London Rifle Brigade* left Shrewsbury with the southbound Pines and worked with the northbound relief Pines the following day. The re-routed Pines (from Shrewsbury) through Wellington was scheduled for a Warship from Crewe, but the first service of the summer was hauled by Oxley Castle 5026 *Criccieth Castle*. The Pines express was re-routed again in 1967 from Manchester to Stoke, Stafford and Wolverhampton, taking it away completely from Wellington.

The Morris Cowley (Oxford) to Bathgate (Glasgow) car trains brought extensive sightings of Britannias on these trains as well as Black Fives.

Freight working through Wellington would see a wide range of both GW- and LM-based locomotives, including the ex-GWR 47XX 2-8-0s, which would be seen on fast freights (usually at night), as well as summer Saturday extra trains.

In 1967, following the allocation of some Western Region Warships to Bescot (near Walsall) depot, they began to appear at Wellington on train no.8J05 working a Bescot to Shrewsbury (Coton Hill), which called at Wellington, where wagons would be detached. For example, on 20 May 1968 no.D852 *Tenacious* worked the train, detaching seven wagons at Wellington, and on 24 May D855 *Triumph* worked the train, depositing twenty wagons at Wellington from its train of forty wagons. Warships continued to work these services throughout 1968 before they left Bescot, having been transferred back to the Western Region.

The end of steam in Shropshire occurred on 4 March 1967, but by this time the Birkenhead to Paddington trains were already diesel-hauled. However, this date also marked the end of the Birkenhead to Paddington trains, as the reopening of a spur just north of Wolverhampton allowed trains from Shrewsbury to run into Wolverhampton High Level and to hand over from diesel traction to electric traction for the run on to Euston.

The services through Wellington were now Shrewsbury to Euston, with diesel haulage (usually a Class 47) as far as Wolverhampton. However, the frequency of the service gradually reduced, until on 10 April 1992 the last through-train ran. In 1997, Virgin Trains started a new Shrewsbury to Euston service, again with a separate diesel locomotive (once more a Class 47) and carriages; however, this was a short-lived service, stopping within three years.

In 2008, a new operator, Wrexham and Shropshire, appeared, starting a new service from Wrexham to Marylebone via Shrewsbury and Wellington, which consisted of Class 67 diesels with separate coaches. Whilst the service was considered excellent, the number of passengers never met expectations and the service ceased on 28 January 2011.

Sulzer Type 4 (later Class 47) at Wellington in June 1964 with a Paddington train. The locomotive is in the demonstration XP 64 livery. Note the ex-LNWR water crane just to the right of the locomotive. UKBUS PHOTOS

Class 37 430 is on the 9.40am from Pwllheli to Euston service at Wellington on 24 June 1989, running sixty-five minutes late. On the left is the 1.28pm Birmingham to Aberystwyth service with Class 150 multiple units. T. HEAVYSIDE

In 2015, Virgin Trains announced that it intended to recommence a Shrewsbury to Euston service using Voyager DMUs. The route was interesting, in that the train would use a newly built junction at Oxley to join the Wolverhampton to Stafford line and the train would then reverse at Stafford to run down the West Coast main line to Euston.

Wellington in the twenty-first century is still recognizable from its steam days and here a Freightliner Class 66 passes through the station. The bay platform still has a single track that is used for permanent way trains and the former loco depot is now a car park. G. CRYER

A Class 47 at Wellington approaches the station with the Washford Heath to Gobowen coal train on 24 June 1989. The signal box on the left was by then the sole remaining signal box in the Wellington area. T. HEAVYSIDE

CHAPTER 3

Madeley Junction to Lightmoor Junction

Madeley Junction to Lightmoor Junction

After leaving Madeley Junction, the line rose on a gradient of 1 in 50, increasing to 1 in 92 near Madeley Court, then falling to 1 in 94, then levelling out before Lightmoor Junction. Prior to reaching Madeley Court, the line passed the sidings for Kemberton Colliery (formerly known as Madeley Wood Colliery) on the left. A single point fanned out into a number of sidings and was controlled from a ground frame.

The Madeley Wood Company operated Kemberton Colliery and the shafts were completed at a depth of 1,092ft (330m) in 1864, but no sidings were put in for the colliery until 1870. By the mid-1880s, regular goods trains worked in and out of the sidings. The four sidings could accommodate ninety wagons. In 1946, three seams were being worked, the Yard, Big Flint and Vigar. During World War II, output varied between 148,675 tons (1944) to 173,132 tons (1941) per annum and in 1946 the annual output was 190,000 tons. The old Halesfield Colliery adjacent to Kemberton was closed in 1925 and joined underground to Kemberton in 1939. It was used thereafter for pumping, ventilation and emergency egress. During 1946, 558 men were employed, but after Nationalization the colliery prospered and the workforce increased to nearly 800. Unfortunately, to the north-east the coal seams were being hampered by geological faults. This severely limited the mine's future and, with a possible extension of the Coalport syncline coal seams east of the Madeley fault not proven, the mine closed in August 1967.

Perhaps the most unusual event on the line was on 19 August 1971, when, after the last coal train of the day had run, a man walking his dog discovered gelignite with a detonator and wiring, in an obvious attempt to blow up the line. The army was called in to make safe the site and the parts were sent away for analysis.

Madeley Court Station

This was the only station between Madeley Junction and Lightmoor Junction and was opened on 2 May 1859. The station was renamed Madeley (Salop) in June 1897 to differentiate it from the nearby LNWR station at Madeley Market. The station was more usually referred to as Madeley Court due to its proximity to the country house of that name. The station was closed for passengers on 22 March 1915, but was reopened for a short period between 13 July 1924 and 21 September 1925 before final closure. The line, from being single, was doubled through the station and there was a small goods yard with a stone-built goods shed, as well as a siding servicing Madeley Court Ironworks.

The station originally had a signal box of nineteen levers opened in 1892, but this was closed in 1899 and was replaced by two ground frames, a covered one east next to the goods yard and west

Madeley Court looking towards Lightmoor Junction with the bridge for the Coalport branch in the distance behind the road overbridge. The covered ground frame can be seen on the right and the siding on the far left goes down to Madeley Court Ironworks. A.J.B. DODD

between the station and the bridge for the Coalport line. This controlled the crossover and the points that served Madeley Court Ironworks and these would be unlocked by the key held by the train crew.

Madeley Court Ironworks was also connected by tramways to Madeley Court Colliery. The siding for the Madeley Court Ironworks was on a gradient down from the line through the station. The ironworks were still receiving coal shipments in the 1960s as part of a pick-up freight service.

Leaving Madeley Court station, the line passed under the LNWR Coalport branch, which crossed the line by an overbridge that was subsequently demolished after the closure of the Coalport branch.

After leaving Madeley Court, the line joined the Wellington to Buildwas line at Lightmoor Junction.

Operating the Line

Whilst the GW passenger services ran, the train started at Wellington and ran to Shifnal via Ketley

The ex-GWR station at Madeley in 1948, which had its passenger service withdrawn in 1925, but goods traffic continued into the 1960s. D. CLARKE

and Lightmoor. There it would reverse to then proceed to Lightmoor Junction to Madeley Court, then running via Madeley Junction to Shifnal (on the main line to Wolverhampton). In 1863, there were five down passenger trains to Wellington, but only two started from Shifnal, with the other three starting at Madeley Court. The working instructions in 1863 for the trains from Shifnal stated that there must be two brake vans at either end of the train to allow reversal at Lightmoor and there must be two guards on the train. Because of the steep gradients on the line, if a passenger train had more than eight carriages and two brake vans, an additional brake van had to be attached to the train.

In the 1860s, there were freights from Shifnal to Lightmoor Junction and Madeley Court to Wellington and of course this was before there were any timetabled freights to and from Kemberton Colliery.

After the opening of the sidings at Kemberton, the empty coal wagons for Kemberton Colliery arrived on a 9.30am train from Hollinswood Yard, but, rather than reversing at Madeley Junction, the locomotive would push the wagons to Kemberton Colliery sidings. The station porter from Madeley Court would meet the train at the colliery sidings and the train crew would unlock the frame and the porter would then operate the ground frame. Upon

In 1955, a rail tour was run through Shropshire, with the last Dean Goods 0-6-0 tender engine, no.2516. Here, the rail tour is seen at Buildwas Junction on 23 April 1955. The train also worked down the Coalport branch. B.K.B. GREEN

completion of shunting and once the engine and train were clear of the points, the train crew would lock the ground frame and the porter would walk back to Madeley Court. The station porter's job operating the ground frame and the walk to and from Madeley Court were not to be envied in harsh winter conditions of driving rain or snow.

If further empties were required at the colliery, the 1.50pm Oxley to Hollinswood would leave them at Madeley Junction, to be picked up by the Shifnal to Buildwas freight and propelled to the colliery. The *Working Time Table* for 1936/7 states that the wagons should be propelled except during foggy weather and falling snow. Presumably in these circumstances the train would have to reverse at Madeley Junction. The *Working Time Table* also shows that some of the empty trains for Kemberton would have loaded coal wagons for Buildwas, but these loaded wagons would be shunted out of the train and left at Madeley Junction.

Although Madeley Court station was closed for passengers, it was a busy station for both goods and parcels. Both the station and goods yard were lit by oil lamps and they remained in use until freight services stopped in 1964. Despite there being no passenger services, there were five staff allocated

to the station including a station master, whose post was only removed in 1934. Parcels traffic for the station was collected at Shifnal, then brought to Madeley Court on the 6.15pm Oxley to Buildwas freight, presumably in the guards van.

Motive power on these passenger and freight trains in the 1880s were 645 Class 0-6-0 saddle tanks and the 655 Class 0-6-0 tender engines. In 1902, no.2076 of the 2021 Class was allocated at Wellington and engines of this class were found at Wellington until the mid-1940s. From the 1930s onwards, the ubiquitous 0-6-0 pannier tanks of various classes would be seen on the local freights.

The grand opening of the Buildwas Power Station (also known as Ironbridge) in October 1932 by the then Minister of Transport required a special train and this was hauled by a Dean Goods 0-6-0 with three saloon coaches and a dining car – a very grand train for a backwater of the railway system.

Although the power station had been opened in 1932, there was still major work outstanding with additional generation units to install, so there was an unadvertised passenger train from Wellington listed in the *Working Time Table* for 1936/7 as 'Workman's Train', departing Wellington for Buildwas at 5.40am. Presumably this service ran

A coal train for Buildwas/Ironbridge A Power Station passes over the Royal Albert Bridge with a Manor 7821 at the head from Oxley shed. In the background the construction of the Ironbridge B can be seen. A.J.B. DODD

until 1939, when construction work ceased and the power station was operating at full design capacity.

The power station was designed to burn Midland slack and this came from a number of sources, with slack trains from the Midlands routed through Oxley Sidings and Madeley Junction, while some from South Wales came via Shrewsbury and down the Severn Valley line. The commencement of open-cast mining at Horsehay Common in 1942 generated a daily coal train from Horsehay to Buildwas. The bulk of the coal came from Granville Colliery via the company's own internal lines to Hollinswood Yard and Madeley Junction. After the closure of the Lilleshall Company's internal railways system, the coal went down to the LNWR line at Donnington, then to Wellington and onwards to Madeley Junction.

In the BR period, the coal trains for Buildwas were hauled by pannier tanks from Wellington, or Shrewsbury would provide 8F 2-8-0s, but from 1964 onwards Oxley shed was responsible for the motive power and a large variety of locomotives could be seen, including BR Standard Class 4s of both 4-6-0 and 2-6-0 configuration, as well as 8F 2-8-0s and on rare occasions a Manor 4-6-0.

When Buildwas Power Station installed the new-style bunkers, the coal trains moved from the 16-ton mineral wagons to HAA hoppers operating as a 'merry go round' train that was air-braked and did not require brake vans. Once Granville Colliery closed in 1976, coal for the power station was sourced from Silverton Colliery near Stoke-on-Trent, then later coal was sourced from the Liverpool Bulk Coal Terminal. In subsequent years, the coal traffic was supplemented by biomass from Liverpool in containers, the power station burning both coal and biomass to reduce its emissions.

In addition to the coal traffic, Buildwas A Power Station also burned oil, so oil tanker trains worked to the power station via Madeley Junction. The responsibility for motive power for these oil trains was usually Bescot and certainly in 1967 Class 24 diesels were seen on the oil train.

With the demise of steam in February 1967, the trains were hauled by a variety of diesels, usually a pair of Class 20s or a Class 47. The most unusual sighting was in 1971 when over a three-day period (9 to 11 August) Class 50 diesels, nos 412, 411 and 425 respectively, worked train 6L42, the Silverdale (Stoke) to Buildwas Power Station coal trains.

A Class 47 196 passes the Coalbrookdale site with a loaded hopper train for Buildwas Power Station on 14 April 1978. T. HEAVYSIDE

In later years, Class 56 and Class 58 diesels were used and today it is the ubiquitous Class 66. One of the Class 58s, 58042 on 29 September 1986, was named *Ironbridge Power Station* at a ceremony at Buildwas, but the locomotive was rarely seen on the power station trains after its naming. The nameplates were moved to another member of the class, 58005, on 12 May 1996.

With the demise of steam in 1967, the Buildwas Power Station trains became diesel-hauled, initially by pairs of Class 20s as seen here on 9 October 1989 with 20 001 and 20 016, the coal now transported in 'merry-go-round' hoppers. D. CLARKE

CHAPTER 4

The Ex-LNWR Line to Stafford

The Wellington to Stafford line was authorized by Act of Parliament on 3 August 1846 and opened in June 1849, having been built by the Shropshire Union Railway. The Shropshire Union was absorbed by the London and North Western Railway in 1847. The LNWR considered the route to be an important one, as it enabled the company to have through coaches from Euston to Shrewsbury, Swansea, Mid Wales, the Cambrian coast and south to Hereford. The route also enabled the company to tap into the East Shropshire coal field and its associated ironworks, as well as freight through to Shrewsbury.

Whilst the staple fare on the line was stopping trains between Stafford and Shrewsbury, the LNWR and subsequently the LMS would also run express trains on the route.

The Wellington to Stafford Line

After leaving Wellington station still on the GW/ LNWR joint line and passing under a road bridge, Stafford Junction was reached with Wellington no.1 signal box on the right. The double track junction curved away to the left. The line to Stafford was singled in July 1971 and removed in 1994, but has subsequently been reinstated as a single track.

Almost immediately after clearing the junction, on the right was Haybridge Iron Company (later known as Haybridge Steel Company), which had a siding and a connection from this siding into the works. The Haybridge Iron Company dated from 1864 and specialized in the production of forging rods, which were used in the manufacture of wire. These sidings were only taken out of use in 1965. As mentioned elsewhere, the Haybridge Iron Company also had a connection on the other side of the works on to the GW main line.

Hadley Station

This was a modest affair, with no goods facilities.

Sankey Works

After leaving Hadley station on the left was the large Sankey works, which had interchange sidings and access directly into the works. Hadley as a community dates back to Saxon times and Hadley Park Mill was powered by both water and steam power. The station was a modest affair.

The Sankey works were formerly known as the Castle Ironworks, which originally made wire, but closed in 1886. In 1902, the site was taken over by G.F. Milnes and Co. of Birkenhead, manufacturing tramcars, and the site became known as Castle Car works. There is a photo showing a train of tramcars loaded on to special wagons leaving the works behind an LNWR 0-6-0 tender engine for Blackburn Corporation. The tram-making business on this site was short-lived, as it closed down in 1908.

The works lay derelict for a few years, until in 1910 the site was taken over by Joseph Sankey and Co. By 1911, Sankey was producing wheels

8F 2-8-0 48735 runs through Hadley station in 1961 with a coal train and shows the modest station building. *H.B. PRIESTLEY*

Hadley Junction marked the location where the ex-LNWR branch line to Coalport diverged from the Wellington to Stafford main line and the adjacent Castle Car works, which originally made tramcars, but moved on to make pressings for the motor industry and armoured personnel carriers for the Ministry of Defence. *D. CLARKE*

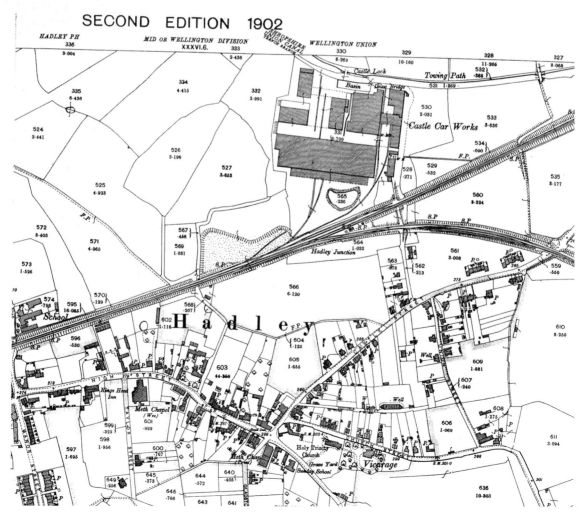

and pressings for car bodies. During the war, the company produced field kitchens, steel helmets, mortar bombs and shell bodies. In 1920, Joseph Sankey became part of the GKN Group.

In the 1930s, the plant was a major producer of car wheels and a range of steel furniture. During World War II, the company produced wheels for military vehicles, steel helmets as well as bomb casings and mines.

Between 1962 and 1972, the company produced 3,000 armoured personnel carriers, the FV430 and variants. The only photograph the author has of the sidings adjacent to the works shows what looks like the shells of the vehicles arriving by rail, but there is no evidence that the completed vehicles left by rail. It is interesting that rail traffic ceased at the same time as this major contract was completed. Certainly other raw materials would have arrived by rail into the works.

The company's first recorded steam locomotive was a Peckett 0-6-0 saddle tank, which was scrapped some time in 1938. During World War II, the Lilleshall Company loaned a Peckett 0-4-0 saddle tank to Sankey, but the locomotive was maintained by Lilleshall Company fitters from Priors Lee Furnaces, who would visit the Sankey works.

In the 1940s, two John Fowler diesel mechanical locomotives joined the works, both coming from the Ministry of Supply Royal Ordnance Factory at Kirkby, Lancashire. Subsequently in 1958, a North British 0-4-0 diesel hydraulic locomotive (built in 1954) arrived and remained at the works until withdrawal, but is now preserved at the Horsehay Steam Trust in Telford. In 1968, another diesel arrived, a 0-4-0 diesel mechanical Hudswell Clarke locomotive built in 1954, the locomotive arriving from another GKN site at Cwmbran. In 1972, rail traffic in and out of the Sankey works ceased.

Hadley Junction

Immediately opposite the Sankey works was the junction for the Coalport line, curving away to the right with a signal box in the 'V' of the junction.

The ex-LNWR line to Coalport left the Wellington to Stafford line at Hadley Junction and the junction can be seen here in 1964. On the left is the GKN Sankey works and its rail access. In the 1960s, Sankey constructed a large number of armoured vehicles for the British Army.
D. CLARKE

After leaving Hadley Junction, Trench Sidings were passed with a signal box to the left and the sidings to the right.

Trench Sidings, the Wombridge Branch and the Trench Inclined Plane

The Shropshire Union built a branch of the Stafford main line in 1866 to service a number of iron-works, including Trench Ironworks, the Shropshire Ironworks and Wombridge Ironworks, as well as other industrial works. The branch also served a canal basin at the foot of the Trench Inclined Plane. The line continued into Wombridge, but this extension past the Trench and Shropshire Ironworks was abandoned in 1873 when the works in the Wombridge area were better served by sidings off the Coalport branch.

With the truncation of the Wombridge branch, the lines serving the Trench and Shropshire Ironworks were expanded and sidings also served a horse nail manufacturer and a chemical works that had previously been a slagworks operated by the Lilleshall Company from 1902. The site then produced phosphate fertilizer and later become Russells Rubber works, which made oil seals, gaskets and rubber flooring. The Shropshire Ironworks had in 1901 thirty-nine puddling and other furnaces, two steam hammers, plus wire and hoop mills. In 1873, drawing and galvaniz-·ing mills had been erected for the manufacture of brass, copper and steel wire, with output measured at between 500 to 600 tons per week, all of which would have left via the railway. According to local tradition, much of the Empire was fenced off by

The 1902 OS map shows the cluster of ironworks adjacent to the canal basin at Trench and the Inclined Plane. The former continuation to the Wombridge Ironworks can be seen and the new connection to the works from the Coalport branch. At the bottom left, the Hadley Brick and Tile works (Blockley's) can be seen.

Trench Lock ran into a canal basin adjacent to an ironworks and the basin was also rail-connected. A view looking towards the Stafford to Wellington line, with the gatepost and level crossing over the Donnington to Hadley Road just visible to the left, where the sidings ran from Trench Sidings on the main line.
IRONBRIDGE GORGE MUSEUM TRUST

wire made by the company. The works continued in production until 1931. The Shropshire Ironworks produced blooms of wrought iron from pig iron for making wire. In 1872, there were twenty-four puddling furnaces and three rolling mills at the Shropshire Ironworks.

The sidings had a small locomotive depot with a single locomotive allocated and the yard was controlled by an LNWR signal box, Trench Sidings. One of the sidings was under the ownership of the Lilleshall Company until 1941, when it came under the control of Shropshire Associated Collieries and from 1949 the National Coal Board.

The Lilleshall Company operated as coal merchants throughout Shropshire (and also in Dudley in the West Midlands) and this siding was part of their domestic coal sales. In one of the few photographs of the site, a set of coal weighing scales can be seen adjacent to the siding and in another photograph a Lilleshall Company wagon can also be seen.

The sidings and engine shed remained covered in weeds until the mid-1960s as Summerfields, a fabrication company, had taken over the site of Trench Ironworks and traffic was worked in and out as required, which was not often.

The interchange sidings at Trench Sidings were controlled by an ex-LNWR signal box called Trench Sidings and is here seen looking towards Trench Crossing station and beyond to Donnington and Stafford. The derelict single road loco shed can be seen on the right. D. CLARKE

The line at Trench Sidings curved round from the main line before crossing the Donnington to Wellington road and continuing to the canal basin and the ironworks. This is a view towards the loco shed and shows the crossing gates on the main road. A small weighbridge can be seen in the foreground, which restricted the weight of any loco working over it. D. CLARKE

The locomotive shed at Trench Sidings in the 1930s, with ex-L&Y 0-4-0 Pug 11218 with a Black Five passing on the line from Stafford. The L&Y 0-4-0 was substituting for the usual ex-Caledonian 0-4-0 saddle tank. W.A. CAMWELL

The locomotive shed at Trench closed in 1943, but remained standing until the mid-1960s, before being swept away in the development of Telford New Town. The track in the foreground leads from the main line to the fabrication company that occupied the site where the ironworks was located. R. CARPENTER

The Trench Inclined Plane was the last working inclined plane in the country. It ceased operation in 1921, having been built in 1793 to service the Shrewsbury Canal and at the top the Wombridge Canal. Small metal tubs were hauled up the inclined plain, then floated on the canal at the top.

Bridge no.62, which crossed the canal behind the loco shed to feed the canal basin, had girders cast by the Lilleshall Company, with the name proudly displayed, but the bridge was removed when the whole site was redeveloped and it is now a large roundabout. As the railway was on the level and crossed over the canal, a lock was required to bring the canal up to the same level as the railway in the canal basin. This was called Trench Lock, but the canal fell into disuse and by the 1950s was clogged with weeds.

After passing Trench Sidings, the line went over a bridge over the canal that serviced the canal basin and reached Trench Crossing station.

In LNWR days, the shunter allocated to Trench Sidings was a small 0-4-0 saddle tank and this photo possibly shows the loco, 3240, allocated to Trench and part of a Shropshire-based private owner wagon, possibly Shropshire Iron Company. D. CLARKE

Trench Crossing Station

A modest station, Trench Crossing opened on 1 January 1855 with a level crossing at the Stafford end of the platform that was controlled by a ground frame on the station platform. The station had gas lamps and these remained in use until the station closed in September 1964. The author can remember the hiss they made when he was waiting for a train in the early 1960s.

Trench Crossing station was a modest affair and remained intact long after the closure of the passenger service in 1964. Here, taken in 1970, the tracks remain in use for the coal trains from Donnington (Granville Colliery) and for the MoD Depot, also at Donnington. The crossing keeper had a peaceful life at this time as there were few trains. D. CLARKE

Trench Crossing looking towards Hadley and Wellington in 1960. The signal box for Trench Sidings can be seen in the distance. Note the gas lamps, which still worked. D. CLARKE

After leaving Trench Crossing, it was a short distance to the signal box on the left controlling access into the Central Ordnance Depot at Donnington. The signal box was built just before World War II and was of a modernist brick and concrete construction with a flat concrete roof.

Central Ordnance Depot, Donnington

The Central Ordnance Depot was started in 1938 and opened in 1939. It had extensive sidings connected to the Stafford to Wellington line. There were seven long sidings with connections at both ends on to the main line, as well as extensive sidings within the depot connected to these interchange sidings. The building progress was slow, but the bombing of London and therefore the threat to the Woolwich Arsenal in East London accelerated the completion and the removal of vital stores away from London. The evacuation from Dunkirk provided further impetus and in 1940 500 railway wagons arrived at Donnington in a period of forty-eight hours, jamming the lines until they had been unloaded and sent away empty. By 1943, transfer from Woolwich had been completed.

The creation of the depot required the building of 844 new houses to accommodate the workers for the site. Donnington was one of three ordnance depots in the country and covered 313 acres (127 hectares), with 8 miles (12.9km) of roads and 12 miles (19.3km) of internal railway line. The depot had nine major equipment and spares stores, with items including field equipment, vehicles and component parts that were dispatched all over the world. The interchange yard was built with a capacity of 700 wagons.

During the war and under the command of Brigadier de Wolff, Donnington grew into a huge depot employing some 15,000 soldiers, 200 members of the Auxiliary Territorial Service (ATS), 2,000 Italian prisoners of war and 4,000 civilians. It was a state of the art storage facility and some of the items supplied included tanks for Russia and some of the first mobile radar units. In modern terms, it was like an Amazon Depot, but without the computer systems to support the staff. Its efficient operation was vital to the war effort and it was working flat out for the duration of the war. As a measure of its importance, the king and queen visited the depot in June 1942. There would have been constant rail movements in and out, particularly in the run-up to the D-Day Landings in June 1944 and afterwards supporting the advance through Europe.

The Central Ordnance Depot at Donnington had its own allocation of army locomotives and these were of the Austerity 0-6-0 type, built in large numbers in World War II. Here, three examples are on-shed in the late 1950s, photographed from a passing Shrewsbury to Stafford train. A.J.B. DODD

The army had extensive sidings at the COD Donnington and there were regular workings into and out of the depot, necessitating a number of shunting locomotives and here three of the army's shunters, nos 420, 427 and 432, sit outside the small locomotive depot at Donnington. The army's standard shunter was the Ruston and Hornsby type seen here in the 1970s. G. CRYER

The Ordnance Depot at Donnington was originally shunted by 0-6-0 saddle tanks of a standard design, of which the army had a large number scattered at its many sites. Here, one of Donnington's is under repair at the small locomotive shed. Some of the depot buildings can be seen in the background. A.J.B. DODD

26 April 1991 saw the ending of the use of army locomotives to shunt the interchange sidings at the COD Depot at Donnington, when the remaining line to Wellington was closed. Here, Army 432 performs its last duties before being moved away. G. CRYER

After the war, the scale of activities reduced, though the depot remained a vital part of the army's logistics. Finished vehicles like tanks were no longer transported by rail, as the latest tanks, such as the Comet and later the Chieftain, were too wide for the British loading gauge, so were transported by road.

With the closure of the line to Stafford in 1964 and the end in 1979 of freight workings from Donnington carrying coal from Granville into Buildwas, the only freight on the line was for the depot. Access from Wellington continued until 1991, with a 08 shunter from Wellington working into the depot and returning any wagons to Wellington, where they could be added to other freight trains. Following the cessation of rail traffic into the depot, the line from Stafford Junction to the depot was removed.

However, from 2001 various proposals were made to reinstate the line to Donnington and in 2009 the Telford International Rail Freight Park was opened, which also allowed traffic for the depot. Traffic has been very light, with trains being run as and when required. All military traffic is now containerized, so that the cargoes cannot be identified.

Donnington Station

Having passed the Ordnance Depot, Donnington station came next. Again there were modest facilities with a level crossing at the Stafford end of the platform. Donnington no.1 signal box (built in 1881) controlled the crossing and Donnington no.2 (also built in 1881) controlled the extensive interchange yard for Granville Colliery and for Walker's Ironworks, whose huge corrugated iron building loomed over the station. As well as the curved sidings for the Lilleshall Company, there were sidings on both the up and down main line.

The Lilleshall Company also had a line that left the interchange sidings and went parallel to the LNWR line, before diving under it to reach the Lubstree Canal wharf. Originally there was a tramway connecting the canal and Lodge Furnaces, but this was converted to a railway in 1870. Limestone for the Lilleshall Company came to the wharf by canal and was then trans-shipped to rail. The Lilleshall Company outstationed a locomotive to shunt the yard adjacent to the canal and bring wagons back to the exchange sidings at Donnington. The Lilleshall Company stopped

View of Donnington station looking towards Wellington, with the interchange with Granville Colliery just in front of the signal box. D. CLARKE

View of Donnington station looking towards Newport showing the ex-LNWR signal box. To the right behind the station is Walkers Ironworks. D. CLARKE

using this line to the canal in 1924 and it was cut back to the exchange sidings.

Walkers Ironworks at Donnington

C. & W. Walker's (also known as Midland Ironworks) was an ironworks company adjacent to Donnington station. It opened in 1857 and had an interchange with the LNWR main line. The works featured a very large corrugated iron building immediately behind Donnington station. By 1900, the business employed 800 people and manufactured gasholders, valves and pressure regulators. Like most heavy industries during World War II, it manufactured items for the war effort, specializing in steel plates for ship construction, gun shields for large guns and bomb casings.

The company had a single steam shunter to work the traffic in and out of the works. The locomotive fleet over the years was as follows:

- *Hale*, a Manning Wardle 0-4-0 saddle tank built in 1888. It was purchased by Walker's in 1895 and scrapped in 1945
- *Westminster*, a Manning Wardle 0-4-0 saddle tank built in 1897, purchased in 1914 and scrapped in 1952
- *Becontree*, a Hudswell Clarke build of 1925, purchased in 1938 and sold in 1952.

C. & W. Walker's, which had a factory adjacent to Donnington station, also had a couple of small industrial locomotives for internal working and for moving finished items to the adjacent LNWR yard. Here, an advert for the products of the company is seen along with one of its locomotives, in this case called Hale.
D. CLARKE

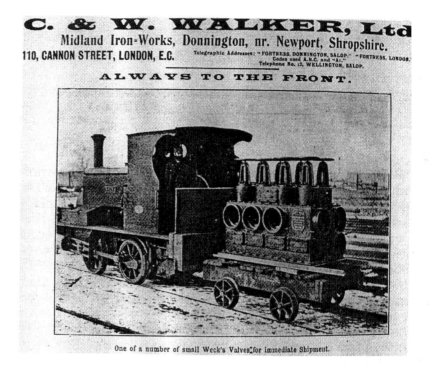

After the last steam locomotive left in 1952, any shunting within the works yard was carried out by a tractor. The sidings into the works were removed in 1977. The works buildings survived until the 1990s, when they were demolished and a housing estate built on the site.

Granville Colliery Interchange Sidings

Sidings curved away from the main line to the right and were originally built for the Lilleshall Company to bring coal from Granville Colliery and iron from Lodge Ironworks for onward shipment to customers. Trains would be worked into the interchange sidings by Lilleshall Company locomotives and the trains would then be taken over by the LNWR. At the Granville Colliery end of the sidings, when they had come down to a single track they passed over the main road controlled by a set of crossing gates that would be operated manually by the locomotive crew of the Granville train. This would take some time, causing great inconvenience to road users.

Granville no.5 (now fitted with Geisel ejector) at Donnington with a loaded coal train. The loco is pushing the train over the level crossing into the interchange, where the train will be picked up by a BR locomotive for onward movement to Buildwas Power Station. D. CLARKE

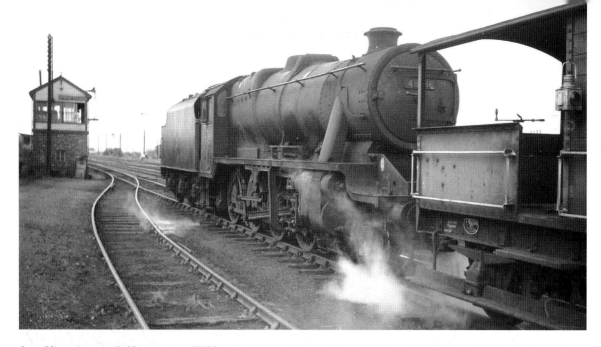

One of Shrewsbury shed's 8F locomotives, 48436, waits in the interchange sidings at Donnington in 1965 for a loaded coal train to arrive from Granville Colliery. The 8F will then work the train to Buildwas Power Station via Wellington and Madeley Junction, which will involve two reversals. D. CLARKE

Operating the Line

LNWR Workings

Stafford and Shrewsbury were the sheds that were the principal suppliers of motive power for both passenger and freight on the line.

In the LNWR summer timetable for 1910, the 8.35am from Euston had five LNWR carriages for Shrewsbury and three Cambrian Railways carriages destined for Aberystwyth. The combined coaches would then be worked as one train from Stafford at 12.40pm to Wellington, where the train would be divided. The LNWR Shrewsbury coaches would leave Wellington at 1.10pm, with the Cambrian coaches following at 1.15pm, bypassing Shrewsbury station by using the Coleham loop.

Similarly, again in the 1910 timetable, the 1.40pm train from Stafford would have the following coaches: one (LNWR) from Birmingham to Aberystwyth; three coaches (two LNWR and one Cambrian) London to Aberystwyth; two coaches (one LNWR and one Cambrian) London to Barmouth; one coach (LNWR) London to Swansea; two coaches (LNWR) Birmingham to Swansea; and one coach Stafford to Swansea (LNWR). Again, the train would be divided at Wellington. The Cambrian portion (for Aberystwyth and Barmouth) would leave Wellington at 2.11pm and bypass Shrewsbury via the Coleham loop, while the Central Wales portion (Swansea) would leave Wellington at 2.40pm and go to Shrewsbury. Given the loadings on both trains and the need to divide the train at Wellington, it is likely that the trains would have been double-headed to Wellington, so that the two locos could then pull the separate trains.

The 2.55pm train from Birmingham, once it arrived at Stafford, would have a through carriage for Swansea attached (which would be detached from the 1.20pm from Euston) and the train would then go forward to Shrewsbury at 4.05pm, probably only stopping at Wellington. Some of the expresses would also stop at Newport, but not all.

In the early hours of the morning, the 1.25am from Tamworth would arrive at Stafford with two Cambrian coaches (Tamworth to Aberystwyth), an LNWR coach from Tamworth to Welshpool and two LNWR postal vans for Hereford. Stafford station would add vans from Euston to Merthyr and Hereford, before sending the train onward to Shrewsbury via Wellington.

Ex-LNWR coal engine 0-6-0 28152 shunts on the Coalport branch near Hadley Junction in April 1949. These Victorian engines were once common in the area, but had all been withdrawn by the early 1950s. R. CARPENTER

This is not an exhaustive list of express passenger trains (there would of course be the corresponding return workings, such as the 11.40am from Shrewsbury, which had Shrewsbury to Stafford coaches, Swansea to Stafford, Swansea to London, Welshpool to London and Aberystwyth to London coaches), but it does show how important the Stafford to Wellington to Shrewsbury route was to the LNWR and also the number of through coaches in the summer timetable. The longest through-coach working the author has found was a West Coast Joint Stock carriage from Edinburgh to Taunton.

Freight traffic in LNWR days was also intensive, with the following services given as an example from the 1909 *Working Time Table*:

- Broad Street (London) to Abergavenny Junction (via Shrewsbury); 'Special Express Goods'
- Burton to Shrewsbury (Coleham Yard); beer train classified as fast goods
- Bescot (near Birmingham) to Abergavenny; express goods
- Monument Lane (Birmingham) to Shrewsbury (Coleham Yard).

Coal traffic was important, as follows:

- Abergavenny Junction to Stafford; locomotive coal. Presumably this was coal from the South Wales coalfields
- Bescot to Shrewsbury; locomotive coal.

In addition to these long-distance workings over the route, there were many freight and coal trains between Shrewsbury and Stafford, some of which were classified as 'Special Express Goods'. The local goods between Stafford and Shrewsbury would stop at most of the intermediate stations as far as Wellington, but would then only stop at Alscott Sidings before arriving at Shrewsbury Coleham Yard. There were also coal empties from Shrewsbury to Wednesbury (near Birmingham).

Although of poor quality, this rare photo shows one of the LNWR Webb compounds 2053 at Wellington with a Shrewsbury to Stafford train at the turn of the century. These engines were not a success and many were transferred to Shrewsbury after being replaced by larger 4-4-0 locomotives. D. CLARKE

As well as the commercial freight trains, the 1909 *Working Time Table* also mentions the regular workings of GWR/LNWR Joint Line ballast trains from Shrewsbury to Donnington, plus ballast trains to run as often as required between Stafford and Coalport. The freight trains were in the hands of LNWR 0-6-0 tender engines such as coal engines, DX goods and 'Cauliflowers' and various versions of the LNWR 0-8-0, both simple and compound.

In the 1890s, the Webb 2-2-2 Problem Class engines were seen on passenger trains, as a number were based at both Stafford and Shrewsbury. No.117 *Tiger*, 618 *Princess Alexander* and 1435 *Fortuna* were all observed on trains between Stafford and Shrewsbury.

One of the features of the passenger trains at the turn of the century was the use of Webb Compound locomotives of the Teutonic, Greater Britain and John Hick classes on the Shrewsbury to Stafford and return trains. These had been the principal main-line express locomotives but were not consistent performers, so when Webb retired the new Chief

Mechanical Engineer, George Whale, rapidly built some large, simple 4-4-0 locomotives and the Webb passenger compounds were cascaded down to less exacting services, with a number being reallocated to Shrewsbury.

LMS Workings

In the 1930s, the 1.03pm Stafford to Shrewsbury train was run as an express, usually with only two coaches, one of which was a Euston to Swansea through coach that would be detached at Stafford from a Euston to Liverpool express. The train from Stafford would run non-stop to Shrewsbury (arriving at 2.20pm), where the Swansea through coach would be added to a train that would depart from Shrewsbury and be routed to Swansea via Craven Arms and the Central Wales line.

In the late 1920s, the Welshman Express would slip a coach (for Swansea) at Stafford, which would be attached to a train for Shrewsbury. After World War II and the Nationalization of the railways, the number of through coaches rapidly diminished and

During the 1930s, a two-coach train from Stafford to Shrewsbury would have express power, as a Euston to Swansea through coach was attached at Stafford and this would run to Shrewsbury, where it would be attached to through coaches from Liverpool and Manchester going forward to Swansea via the Central Wales line. Here a Compound 4-4-0 is seen in 1938 between Stafford and Shrewsbury. D. CLARKE

the Stafford to Shrewsbury trains settled into a set of stopping trains.

In the 1930s and 1940s, Stafford shed's ex-LNWR locomotives could be seen on passenger and freight services, with the Bowen Cooke 4-6-2 tanks on the stopping services and the fast through services being worked by Compound 4-4-0s. The Fowler Patriots were also seen on the line. Stafford and Shrewsbury G2 0-8-0s were regularly seen on the line until the early 1960s. Stafford shed also had some of the last surviving ex-LNWR 4-6-0 Prince of Wales Class and no.25648 *Queen of the Belgians* and no.25673 *Lusitania* were regularly seen on passenger services. Certainly Shrewsbury shed's rebuilds of the Prince of Wales Class fitted with outside valve gear, known as 'Tishy' locos, were seen on passenger trains, including 25845, and the 4-4-0 Precursors were also seen on the line.

Stafford shed had the last ex-LNWR Prince of Wales locomotives and here 25648 Queen of the Belgians *is on Stafford shed in August 1948 and the engine was seen regularly on services to Shrewsbury and back until it was withdrawn in October 1948.* M. WHITEHOUSE

A typical Stafford to Shrewsbury train in the early 1960s, with one of Stafford shed's Fowler 2-6-4 tanks, no.42421, on the usual three-coach train. The motive power on these trains was shared between Stafford and Shrewsbury sheds until the line closed to passengers in September 1964. D. CLARKE

British Railways

In the 1950s, the elderly ex-LMS 2P 4-4-0s (including nos 40419 and 40677) could be seen on the Shrewsbury to Stafford services and for the Wellington to Newport service in 1950 ex-LNWR coal tanks (including 58904) were still in use. No.58904 was a Shrewsbury engine, but was regularly used on the Wellington to Coalport services and would therefore be available at Wellington to haul a train to Newport and back.

In the early 1960s, the motive power for the passenger services settled down to a staple fare of locomotives, with Stafford shed's Fowler 2-6-4 tanks (and Fairburn variants), as well as Shrewsbury shed's BR Standard Class 4 4-6-0s (no.75000 through to no.75009), which arrived in 1951. Diagrams 4 and 5 from Shrewsbury had Stafford trains included. However, in 1953 the Standard Class 4 4-6-0s were transferred away and were replaced by the larger BR Standard Class 5 4-6-0s, with 73025, 73090, 73095, 73096 being

regulars. The smaller Class 4s had been found wanting on the trains down the Central Wales line, so were replaced by their larger cousins.

As well as Shrewsbury Standard Class 5s, the shed's Stanier Black Fives and Jubilees (after their arrival at Shrewsbury in October 1961), including nos 45577 *Bengal*, 45660 *Rooke*, 45562 *Kempenfelt* and 45651 *Shovel*, were seen on the trains to Stafford. A variety of Jubilees from Crewe North shed were also observed on these trains. The usual formation of the stopping trains was three ex-LMS coaches, although occasionally four coaches would be used.

Three horseboxes were seen attached to the front of one of these trains at Wellington in March 1964 with a Stanier 2-6-4 tank (no.42542) at the head; again, the why and the wherefore are unknown to the author. Certainly in the 1930s, the GWR ran special trains to the Horse Fair at Wrexham, so there may have been a connection there, but this is speculation.

From the mid-1950s, the passenger services between Shrewsbury and Stafford were regularly pulled by Shrewsbury's Standard Class 5 4-6-0s and here 73036 pauses at Trench station c. 1963 with a train from Stafford. D. CLARKE

In the 1960s, the freight traffic on the Stafford to Wellington section was frequent, with trains to and from Donnington MoD depot, coal trains from Granville Colliery, as well as through freights. Here, an unidentified Black Five in 1964 approaches the platform ends of Trench Crossing in the Stafford direction. D. CLARKE

One of Stafford shed's Fowler 2-6-4 tanks, no.42381, runs into Hadley station with a Stafford to Shrewsbury train. In the background, the Sankey works dominate the skyline. D. CLARKE

Another Stanier 2-6-4 tank, no.42488, was seen on a Stafford train and in the early 1960s a most unusual set of coaches was seen leaving Shrewsbury behind Fairburn 2-6-4 tank no.42224, which consisted of two ex-LNER Thompson coaches and an ex-LNER articulated two-coach set, all in what looked like ex-works condition. How this set of coaches came to replace the usual three coaches of ex-LMS '57 vintage is a complete mystery to the author.

One of the unusual classes of locomotive seen on the Shrewsbury to Stafford and return stopping trains was BR Standard Class 6 Clan Pacific no.72008 *Clan Macleod* in July 1954. The locomotive had been at Crewe works for attention and was then sent to Shrewsbury on a running-in

turn. It then appears that Shrewsbury shed sent it to Stafford and back before the engine returned to Crewe.

However, from the 1950s to 1962, ex-LMS rebuilt Class 7 4-6-0s would be seen on the stopping trains being used on a fill-in turn. The 11.25am Shrewsbury to Stafford would be worked by a Class 7 and upon arrival at Stafford the locomotive would then work to Birmingham. The 3.10pm Shrewsbury to Stafford would be worked by an Edge Hill Class 7, which had arrived at Shrewsbury on a Manchester to Plymouth train. The locomotive would then work back to Shrewsbury from Stafford before picking up an express at Shrewsbury back to the North West. In 1962, the author spotted nos 45531 *Sir Frederick Harrison*, 45535 *Sir Herbert Walker*, 46119

Lancashire Fusilier, 46135 *The East Lancashire Regiment* and 46148 *The Manchester Regiment* at Trench Crossing.

Not only Edge Hill rebuilt Class 7s were seen. In 1954 one of Holyhead's rebuilt Scots, no.46129 *The Scottish Horse*, was seen leaving Shrewsbury with a Stafford train and it appears to have been common practice for Shrewsbury to have sent a Class 7 loco to Stafford and back as a fill-in turn. Examples include nos 46118 *Coldstream Guardsman* of Crewe North, 46124 *London Scottish* of Edge Hill, 46148 *The Manchester Regiment* of Crewe North and 46166 *The London Rifle Brigade*, also of Crewe North. Other motive power seen included Britannia Pacific no.70023 *Venus* on a Stafford to Shrewsbury train.

One of the more unusual engines seen on these services was Southern Region Standard Class 5 no.73087 *Linette*. During the summer, a once a week service from Wolverhampton to the south coast and its return service would effectively strand the Southern Region locomotive in the West Midlands for a week; it seems to have been borrowed by Shrewsbury shed as the loco was seen a number of times. Similarly, the LM Region Black Five from Oxley working the southbound service would be employed by Bournemouth shed on its week's stay.

Crewe North and Burton-on-Trent Jubilees were also seen working the stopping trains. Examples include no.45578 *United Provinces* of Crewe North in 1961 and no.45641 *Sandwich* of Burton shed.

In 1962, larger motive power was seen on the line when, due to engineering work in relation to the electrification of the West Coast main line, parcels traffic was temporarily diverted from Crewe to Market Drayton. The result was that twice a week an empty stock parcels train would work from Market Drayton to Willesden via Wellington and Stafford and, due to the loading (up to twenty vehicles), required a Class 7 or a Class 8 locomotive. Locomotives seen on this train included two Stanier Pacifics (nos 46235 *City of Birmingham* and 46248 *City of Leeds*), a Britannia (70004 *William Shakespeare*) and a 9F 2-10-0. In 1965, some of the parcels workings were transferred to Wellington,

which had a 9.12am Wellington to Willesden empty van train running on Tuesdays, Thursdays and Saturdays. Whilst the loading did not require Class 8 locomotives, a number of Crewe Britannias were observed on this working, including no.70019 *Lightning*. The locomotive would work light-engine from Crewe to Wellington to work the train.

In March 1962, two-car Diesel Multiple Units (DMUs) were used on the line, but these moved away and for the last couple of years the passenger service reverted back to steam.

The freight services were in the hands of G2 0-8-0 and 8F 2-8-0s, with Stanier Mogul 2-6-0s also being seen. Stanier Black Fives were also common and Stafford's Fowler 2-6-4 tanks were seen on pick-up freights. Wellington's pannier tank 0-6-0s were also regulars, both on the Granville coal trains, as well as pick-ups from Wellington to the COD Depot at Donnington. An occasional Sulzer Type 2 (Class 24) was seen on the Granville coal trains. Strangely, given how common Shrewsbury's BR Standard Class 5s were on the line, they do not appear to have been used on freight trains. Sometimes interlopers were seen, for example the author saw Jubilee no.45730 *Ocean* passing the Ordnance Depot in 1963 on a freight and this locomotive was allocated at Warrington.

A number of trains worked in and out of the Ordnance Depot at Donnington, some as through trains and some as trip workings from Wellington. Observed on these trip workings were a number of Wellington's 0-6-0 pannier tanks, plus Shrewsbury's Ivatt Class 2 2-6-0 no.46519 in unlined green livery. Arriving from Wellington, the loco would shunt in the depot yard and then return to Wellington. On arrival at Wellington, the wagons would be resorted and await a train to move them on to their destination.

In the early 1960s, an afternoon freight ran into the Donnington COD Yard from the Wellington direction and was observed hauled by a variety of Black Five 4-6-0s (nos 44829 and 44941), Burton Jubilees, nos 45593 *Kholapur*, 45641 *Sandwich* and 45721 *Impregnable*, rebuilt Scot 46155 *The Lancer* and a Burton 4F. Having dropped off wagons and

A Bescot 8F trundles through Donnington station in 1965 with a freight train. To the right can be seen the tall buildings of Walker's Ironworks and the interchange sidings for the Granville Colliery trains. D. CLARKE

picked up others, the train would then depart in the Stafford direction.

In 1976, when the only traffic on the truncated line to Stafford was the trip working to the depot, a 08 diesel shunter was used to take wagons to Wellington, where they would be resorted and attached to trains.

At various times, the Wellington to Stafford line was used as a diversionary route both by the London Midland Region and Western Region, so in November 1953, because of engineering work on Shifnal Viaduct (between Wellington and Wolverhampton), Western Region trains worked from Wellington to Stafford and reached Wolverhampton via Stafford. Halls and Castles were observed on these trains.

Trains at Crewe could also be diverted to Market Drayton, Wellington and then Stafford to rejoin the West Coast main line. So, as an example on 9 July 1961, a number of expresses headed by Britannias, rebuilt Scots and Jubilees used this diversionary route. The route continued to be used as a diversion route up until the mid-1960s.

In 1959, on the last four Saturdays of the summer service, the 6.35pm from Crewe to Camden Class C express freight (milk and perishables) was routed via Shrewsbury, Wellington and Stafford and the train was observed with no.46150 *The Life Guardsman* from Crewe North (5A), 456433 *Rodney* from Crewe North and 46138 *The London Irish Rifleman*, another Crewe North locomotive. Freight trains on the route also varied, with coal trains from

GW Castle no.5015 Kingswear Castle *threads its way through Stafford station with a diverted Birkenhead to Paddington train, having taken the junction at Wellington and travelled to Stafford via Donnington on 29 November 1953. It will go forward to Wolverhampton and regain the ex-GWR line.* R. CARPENTER

Donnington Exchange Sidings to Buildwas Power Station from 1958, as well as a number of through freights, such as the Burton to Shrewsbury beer trains.

At the end of 1961, Burton shed acquired a large number of Jubilee 4-6-0s from Derby and other passenger depots in the East Midlands and over the period until October 1964 further engines arrived. Burton's Jubilees then appeared regularly on the line on all sorts of freights including beer trains, as well as working freight trains in and out of the Ordnance Depot.

In 1964, the number of freight trains was still extensive, with trains from Stafford to Cardiff, Stafford to Shrewsbury (Coton Hill Yard), Burton (Branston) to Shrewsbury, Burton to Swansea,

Burton to Hereford, as well as the coal trains from Donnington to Wellington and beyond to Buildwas.

With the closure of Wellington shed in August 1964 and other changes, the responsibility for working the coal trains from the interchange yard at Donnington to Buildwas passed from Shrewsbury and Wellington to Oxley shed (Wolverhampton) and a number of different classes appeared, including BR Standard Class 4 4-6-0 (including 75024), Standard Class 4 2-6-0s (including no.76039) and ex-GWR 0-6-2 tank (including no.5606).

In April 1965, the Brush Type 4 diesels were seen on the line with Llandore (South Wales) based engines working light-engine from Shrewsbury to work the 9.45am Stafford to Margam (South Wales) Class 7 train and the 6.10pm Stafford to Llandeilo service. On 4 December 1965, a Football Special from Peterborough to Shrewsbury was routed via the Stafford to Wellington route with a Class 31 D5624 at its head, the first sighting of the class on the line.

With the passing of steam and the closure of the route beyond Donnington in 1967, diesel power was seen on the Buildwas coal trains and trains to the Ordnance Depot at Donnington. The coal trains were worked by diesels from Bescot depot, with Classes 20, 31, 37, 40 and 47 observed on these workings.

With the closure of the colliery in May 1979, the last coal train ran in June 1979, having cleared the remaining coal stocks at Granville. The most unusual visitor on the line, however, was Warship no.D809 *Champion*, still in maroon livery, on 14 September 1967, when it worked a Wolverhampton, Donnington, Newport and back to Wolverhampton Inspection Saloon working. A small number of Warships had been allocated to Bescot depot near Birmingham, where the Inspection Saloon for the district was based. Before steam finished at Bescot, the normal motive power for the Inspection Saloon would have been one of Bescot's Ivatt Class 2 2-6-0s, usually nos 46522 or 46527.

A similar Inspection Saloon working with a Class 47 at the head arrived at Donnington in 1969. The driver came back into the saloon and said he was unsure about proceeding as he could not see the rails because of the undergrowth (the section between Donnington and Newport having been closed earlier in 1969).

Although the route was ex-LNWR and ex-LMS, the *Western Region Working Time Table* for June 1960 stated that the following ex-WR locomotives were authorized to work between Wellington and Donnington:

- Hall 4-6-0 49XX
- Castle 4-6-0 50XX
- Grange 4-6-0 68XX
- Manor 4-6-0 78XX
- 43XX 2-6-0
- 51XX 2-6-2 tanks.

Certainly Castles and Halls were seen in 1953 with diverted Birkenhead to Paddington trains, but the author has no record of any of the other classes working the line, although he would like to be proved wrong!

8F 48699 of 15D Coalville shed runs through Trench Crossing station c. 1963–4. The engine is either returning to its home shed after overhaul at Crewe works, or is on its way to Donnington to pick up a coal train from Granville Colliery. A.J.B. DODD

CHAPTER 5

The Coalport Branch

As with many of the lines in the Telford area, the railway to Coalport started life as a canal, with the Shropshire Canal running down to Coalport. The majority of the traffic did not travel far and some freight was trans-shipped on to the River Severn. The LNWR leased the canal from 1849, but always had the intention of creating a railway line and in 1857 gained authorization from Parliament to purchase the canal and convert it to a railway. Construction started in 1858 and opened for freight in 1860. The passenger service started on 10 June 1861 with all the stations being opened on the same day except for Malins Lee station, which did not open until 7 July 1862. The stations had a pleasing uniformity and this was partially due to all of them being built by the same local building company.

Like many lines constructed at this time, the ballast was of ashes and cinders and even into the 1960s cinder ballast could still be found on the line. The use of ash and cinder ballast was helped by the plentiful supply from the various ironworks and brickworks in the area.

The line was built as a single line with passing loops and was operated by the staff and ticket method. The train staff given to the driver gave him the authority to proceed on a single-line section and the staffs could be issued at Hadley Junction, Oakengates, Stirchley and Coalport. This method of working therefore meant that there was only one signal box on the line, at Oakengates. The various ground frames dotted along the line to access yards and sidings would be worked either by train crew or by station staff.

One of the key features of the line was the steep descent down to Coalport from Malins Lee, with a gradient of 1 in 50 going down to 1 in 40 for the last mile to the station. Plans were drawn up for the line to continue past Coalport station, cross the River Severn and make a junction with the Severn Valley line, but like so many proposals in the mid-1850s this was never constructed.

The Coalport Branch Line

Having left Wellington, the Coalport trains would take the Stafford line at Stafford Junction, stopping at Hadley before turning right from the Stafford line at Hadley Junction. This was a two-track junction, but the branch became single after a few hundred yards. The signal box was rebuilt in 1906 and between the junction and where the branch became a single line, there were several goods sidings acting as interchange yards as a number of freight trains started and terminated in these sidings.

Soon after leaving the junction there were sidings on the right serving the Hadley Brick and Tileworks, better known as Blockley's. The sidings appeared to have been in use by 1897 and were controlled by a small ground frame. The sidings changed over the years, with additions in 1925. The company is still in operation, although it was sold in

2013 to Bovis Homes, who will build houses on part of the site but the brickworks will continue.

After passing Blockley's connection, there were sidings on the left providing access into the Wombridge Ironworks, which produced pig iron. In the 1870s, the site became a forge, with ten puddling furnaces producing wrought iron that was rolled in three rolling mills. The Wombridge Ironworks had previously been accessed by the Wombridge branch from Trench Sidings, but this was shortened in the 1870s and the works accessed from the Coalport branch.

After the connection into Wombridge Ironworks was passed on the left, a few hundred yards on the right was Wombridge Ballast Tip Sidings, which were added in 1912. The sidings were constantly moved as the area adjacent to the track was filled with spent ballast. The land used for dumping the waste was formerly Wombridge Pool. Wombridge Ballast Tip Sidings were removed sometime between 1937 and 1940, presumably as the location had become full. One of the operational issues that all railways faced was how to dispose of spent ballast without having to transfer it many miles, so local dumping facilities were important.

After passing the ballast tip sidings, the next connection was on the left, servicing a quarry that appeared to be opened in 1874 and had a ground frame. The connection had been removed by 1902 and the OS map for that date has the site as 'Old Quarry'.

Oakengates Market Street Station

The first station was at Oakengates, which had a passing loop and two sets of platforms. The sidings adjacent to the station had two goods sheds and a siding into a sawmill and timber yard owned by Millington's. The Millington timber yard was also

A view of Oakengates Market Street in the early 1960s just before closure, with the Lilleshall Company's Snedshill works on the horizon to the right. D. CLARKE

View looking towards Wellington at Oakengates Market Street station in 1932 showing the level crossing, an ex-LNWR signal and the shortened platform on the down side. The signal box was the only one on the branch. D. CLARKE

A view of Oakengates on the Coalport branch looking towards Wellington, showing the falling gradient through the station, with the goods yard on the level. A.J.B. DODD

accessed from the Great Western main line, with a siding from the goods yard at Oakengates station that was only a short distance away from the LNWR station. There was a small signal box on the down platform that was the only signal box on the line. The second platform on the down side was taken out of use in the 1950s and the down loop was then only used by freight trains.

Just south of Oakengates, there was an interchange with the Snedshill Ironworks (which later became part of the Lilleshall Company and subsequently John Maddox and Co.). There were four sidings fanning out from the points on to the Coalport branch to allow the sorting of inbound and outbound goods from the site. Snedshill Ironworks had been opened as early as 1770 with blast furnaces by John Wilkinson, but had closed by 1830. The site then reopened as a forge and rolling mill and was then acquired by the Lilleshall Company. In the 1900s, the two adjoining sites were rationalized, with iron and steel produced at Priors Lee and wrought iron at Snedshill. The Snedshill Ironworks

closed in 1925 and shortly afterwards the site was bought by John Maddox and developed into one of the most modern casting foundries in Europe.

An unusual feature of the line was the placement of a loading gauge on the branch line opposite the sidings for Snedshill in the 1950s. The assumption is that the branch at this time was operated as a long siding. Loading gauges would not normally be placed on a running line, only in a siding.

A little further on was a set of sidings for an interchange with the Lilleshall Company's Priors Lee Steelworks. Beyond the interchange with the Lilleshall Company there was an interchange with the Eagle Ironworks, but this was removed in 1895. Opposite the Eagle Ironworks was a siding for the Stirchley Iron and Coal Company that was removed in 1927.

On the left was a brickworks crammed into the narrow space between the GWR main line and the Coalport branch, but the works was not connected to the Coalport branch. On the opposite side were the spoil tips of the closed Old Dark Lane Colliery.

An unusual working on the Coalport branch, with 82031 on what appears to be a gauging train in the sidings for Snedshill Ironworks. The Coalport branch is in the foreground. Note the loading gauge on the running line. A.J.B. DODD

A Coalport to Wellington train is approaching Oakengates Market Street and shows the sidings linked to Priors Lee Ironworks to the right. T.G. WASSELL

Malins Lee Station

The next station was at Malins Lee, which had a single platform and sidings servicing Dark Lane Foundry, but these sidings were removed in the 1950s. On the left-hand side of the line the landscape was dominated by spoil tips from a number of disused collieries including Little Dark Lane, Lodge Colliery and Wharf Colliery. These had all closed by the beginning of the twentieth century. The majority of the spoil consisted of Pennystone Clay, which also contained iron ore; this spoil was worked by gangs of women recovering the iron ore.

Soon after leaving Malins Lee station, a short siding curved away to the left to access Randlay Brickworks. This short siding crossed a reservoir via a causeway before reaching the works. The brickworks was also accessed from the other side by the Great Western Stirchley branch (also known as the Old Park branch), so the works could decide with which company to send out their goods, depending on the rates charged.

Before the next station, Stirchley Ironworks had an interchange with the line, via sidings firstly known as Bottfields Sidings, then Hinkshay Sidings. They were taken out of use in February 1957.

Malins Lee station in 1932 with the sidings for Dark Lane Foundry in the distance on the right. The station was built on the site of a canal and the landscape of the area had a rural outlook, but with chimneys that can be clearly seen. The station closed in 1952, before the withdrawal of the passenger services in 1953. D. CLARKE

Malins Lee station after closure of the passenger trains in 1952 taken from the guard's van of a pick-up goods service. A.J.B. DODD

Mineral lines serving both the Ironworks and the Wrekin Chemical works crossed over the Coalport branch and curved round, reaching the sidings just before Stirchley station.

Dawley and Stirchley Station

Stirchley station was renamed Dawley and Stirchley station on 9 July 1923. The line became double track for a short time and the station had two platforms, but like Oakengates the down platform had been taken out of use by 1902. There was a ground frame on the platform that was active from 1902, having replaced one at the end of the platform installed in 1891. Stirchley also had two sidings and a goods shed. The sidings were taken out of use in May 1954.

Madeley Market station

The next station was Madeley Market, which again originally had two tracks through the station with two platforms, but the second platform and track were removed in 1915. There was a small yard behind the station with three sidings controlled by a small ground frame at the yard throat.

Before Coalport was reached, there were sidings to J. Legge Brickworks (removed in 1959), then an interchange with Blists Hill Ironworks. After the Ironworks closed in 1912, the siding was used by Madeley Wood Company, and was removed in 1952.

This OS map of 1902 shows the Randlay Brickworks connected to both the Coalport branch on the left and the Stirchley branch on the right. Also shown are the spoil tips for the derelict collieries.

Dawley and Stirchley station (renamed from Stirchley) is seen here in 1932 looking towards Wellington, with the station already reduced to a single platform. The former goods yard can be seen curving away to the right behind the telegraph poles. D. CLARKE

Madeley Market station in 1932.
D. CLARKE

Further down the track there was another siding for the Madeley Wood Company (removed in 1952).

On the approach to Coalport station there was a siding into the Coalport China Company controlled by a ground frame. The Coalport factory relocated to Stoke-on-Trent in 1926 and the works were taken over by Nu-way MFG.

Coalport Station

Coalport had a single platform, plus a small carriage and locomotive shed. When the line was opened there was an interchange with the river to allow goods to be trans-shipped on to river barges, but by 1902 this interchange was no longer operational, although the small yard remained in use until 1960. The run-round loop and yard were controlled by a ground frame opposite to the carriage shed and locomotive shed. The carriage shed had two tracks and the locomotive shed originally also had two tracks, but when the retaining wall needed reinforcing the locomotive shed was reduced to one track.

A view of the exterior of Coalport station c. 1910. D. CLARKE

An ex-LNWR coal tank in LMS days sits outside the locomotive shed at Coalport. The shed was originally a two-road affair, but the local subsidence led to the shed being reduced to one road (in 1925), with one of the roads now being occupied with some major reinforcing to ensure that the retaining wall did not collapse. W.A. CAMWELL

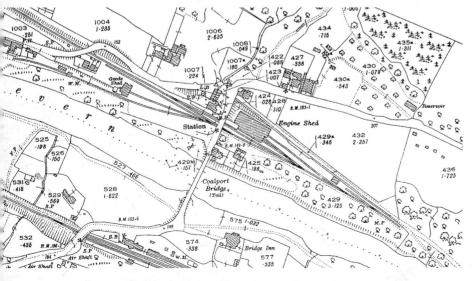

LNWR Coalport station clearly showing the engine shed and the head shunt in 1925. On the opposite side of the river is the GWR station on the Severn Valley line down to Bridgnorth and beyond.

The two- road carriage shed was adjacent to the locomotive depot at Coalport and this March 1955 photos shows the empty building as the passenger service had ceased in 1952. Subsequently the only passenger services from Coalport were occasional excursions.
F.W. SHUTTLEWORTH

After World War II, the carriage shed was much larger than the services required with the same two coaches in use, but this was a reminder of the higher traffic levels in the 1900s.

A brick-built water tower with a metal tank on the top was provided past the locomotive shed. Access to the engine shed and carriage shed was taken out of use in 1962, although by then these sidings were covered in weeds.

Operating the Line

The passenger trains departed from Wellington and after turning on to the line to Stafford at Stafford Junction, they went to Hadley station, before leaving

Fowler 2-6-2 tank 40005 takes on water at the head shunt at Coalport station in the early 1950s. HMRS

G2 0-8-0 49276 arrives at Coalport with a short freight of coal wagons during a misty March 1952. This class of locomotive was seen on the remaining freight workings until they were replaced by 0-6-0 pannier tanks. The coaching stock stands in the adjacent siding. D. CLARKE

the line to Stafford and turning down the branch to Coalport at Hadley Junction. The line measured from Hadley Junction was just 7¾ miles (12.5km) long, but was built essentially for freight traffic. The first passenger trains when the line opened on 10 July 1861 were hauled by the Webb Special Tanks pulling some four-wheeled coaches, but with the steep gradient down to Coalport this proved to be difficult due to inadequate braking, so the coaching stock was changed to six-wheeled coaches with additional braking capacity. The locomotives were soon replaced by 2-4-2 tanks and later by the Webb 0-6-2 coal tanks.

In 1910, the LNWR introduced a two-coach motor train on the branch, each of the coaches being 50ft (16.4m) long and hauled by a 4ft 6in (1.48m) 2-4-2 tank. The motor train could be driven from the opposite end of the train from the locomotive, thus avoiding the need to run round the train at Coalport and Wellington. The LNWR had a number of coaches converted for motor use on its smaller branch lines. The motor trains ran until the 1920s, when the service reverted back to ordinary coaches and locomotives. The coaching stock for the last few years of operation was a pair of wooden-bodied Pre-Grouping coaches, the non-corridor coach being a conversion by the LNWR of two 28ft (9.2m) coaches mounted on a new single underframe and the corridor coach being a 57ft (18.7m) of LNWR origin, built in 1920. Some ex-Lancashire and Yorkshire coaches were seen in the sidings at Coalport in the 1950s, but do not seem to have been used on service

40005 at Coalport with a train for Wellington, with a single elderly ex-LNWR wooden-bodied coach. Why the horsebox is in the train is unknown to the author. D. CLARKE

The LNWR services from Wellington to Coalport were worked by engines allocated to Coalport, a sub-shed of Shrewsbury (shed code 30 seen above the coal in the bunker). Here, coal tank no.549 is seen at the bay platform at Wellington with a train of six-wheeled coaches in 1895. D. CLARKE

Small pannier tank 1663 has disgraced itself and requires heavy lifting power at Oakengates on the Coalport branch. The breakdown train blocks the level crossing, causing inconvenience to the locals. The loco was allocated to Wellington from January 1957 until October 1958.
A.J.B. DODD

trains; if they were, they have not been captured on film.

The line retained some of the original LNWR signals, with later LMS signals also being seen.

In addition to the stations, there were a number of sidings for freight services at Madeley Wood, Old Park Sidings, Randlay Sidings, Priors Lee Sidings (for interchange with the Lilleshall Company), Snedshill Ironworks and Hadley Lodge Sidings, as well as Coalport Factory Sidings. Just after the junction at Wellington were sidings for Haybridge Ironworks and one copy of the *LNWR Working Time Table* shows these sidings listed, although no freight is notified to call there; presumably it was a case of as and when required. The number of private sidings on the line meant that twenty-four diagrams were issued by the LNWR and the LMS to document the various siding interconnections for operating purposes.

The line to Wellington served a number of industrial sites such as Coalport China and a number of brickworks, tileworks, coal, ironstone, pig iron and other industrial enterprises, with five freight workings each way in 1905. In 1909, there were four passenger workings and seven freight workings in each direction. The line suffered a blow in 1926 with the moving of the Coalport factory to Stoke-on-Trent, thereby reducing freight traffic on the branch as the works would have required china clay and coal inwards, as well as finished goods outwards. Private owner wagons from Cornwall bringing in china clay included *North and Rose* and *St Austell China Clay*, as well as coal wagons from Littleton, Baggeridge and Rugeley Collieries. The local collieries wagons from Lilleshall and Madeley Wood were also seen.

Freight traffic into Coalport was also sent to the trans-ship wharf on the River Severn for loading on to boats.

Fowler 2-6-2 tank 40058 of Shrewsbury shed leaves Coalport on the 2.35pm to Wellington on 15 March 1952. D. CLARKE

The *LNWR Working Time Table* also mentions ballast trains to run as often as required between Stafford and Coalport and of course waste ballast was taken to Wombridge Ballast Tip sidings, so after trackwork was completed the waste could be tipped locally.

In 1939, the freight traffic for the branch was still busy, as follows:

- 6.20am goods from Shrewsbury to Coalport (arrive 9.40am); depart Coalport 10.30am for Hadley Junction
- 7.56am goods from Stafford to Priors Lee sidings (arrive 10.15am); depart Priors Lee 10.30am to Stafford (this would require a reversal at Hadley Junction)
- 12.25am minerals from Hadley Junction to Coalport (arrive 1.45pm); depart Coalport 2.50pm Saturday excepted (SX) to Hadley Junction
- 10.20am (SX) goods from Stafford to Priors Lee sidings (arrive at 2.15pm); depart Priors Lee 2.45pm for Stafford (the Saturday only train ran at a slightly different time)
- 4.40pm minerals (SX) from Hadley Junction to Madeley Market (arrive 5.55pm); depart Madeley Market at 6.10pm for Hadley junction.

During World War II, passenger services on the line were reduced and the branch was used as a storage site for ammunition. Special trains were observed behind Black Five 4-6-0s. It is not known to the author where these ammunition stores were on the branch, but it is likely that they were a short-term ad hoc arrangement, as ammunition stores elsewhere in the country had their own internal railway systems and specific storage facilities, and were usually well away from people! As an example, the old Shropshire and Montgomery system was commandeered by the military and special ammunition stores were built out in the countryside.

A Coalport train arrives at the bay platform at Wellington behind Fowler 2-6-2 tank 40005 with its motley collection of ex-LNWR wooden-bodied coaches. These Fowler tanks were the mainstay of the passenger trains to and from Coalport in the last few years of the service.
T.C. COLE

View of one of the last remaining ex-LNWR coal tanks, no.58904, at Coalport in July 1950, with a train to Wellington consisting of the usual pair of elderly ex-LNWR wooden-bodied coaches. The locomotive was allocated to Shrewsbury shed, which was responsible for supplying motive power for the Coalport branch before regional boundary changes. F.W. SHUTTLEWORTH

After the closure of passenger services between Wellington and Coalport on 31 May 1952, freight services continued. A daily pick-up freight (originating from Shrewsbury Coton Hill) worked the full length of the branch, but traffic was declining, although Oakengates was still relatively busy. The train from Shrewsbury would shunt the coal road, removing the empties and placing the loaded coal wagons for the merchants CWS Ltd and Messrs W. Upton and Son. The goods shed was still in use and scrap metal was loaded in the yard. Coke was also brought in for John Maddox (Snedshill Ironworks) of Oakengates from Tonyrefail in South Wales.

The full diagram for the train in 1956 was as follows: 5.35am Shrewsbury to Coalport; 11.10am Coalport to Wellington; 2.30pm Wellington to Priors Lee sidings; 3.53pm return to Shrewsbury. This diagram was known as Target 69.

The relocation of Coalport China and the closure of the Lilleshall Company's blast furnaces at Priors Lee in 1959 meant that freight on the branch continued to decline. After December 1960, the freight

service was cut back to Stirchley. Coal continued to be delivered to W.P. Dawkins & Co. at Dawley and Stirchley, but the line was completely closed on 6 July 1964. In the last days of the freight service, one of Wellington's 0-6-0 pannier tanks was deemed sufficient for the volume of traffic, nos 3739, 4605, 9630 and 9639 all being seen, with no.4605 the regular engine. Wellington for a short time had a few examples of the small pannier class including no.1663, which was allocated there between 1957 and 1958 and was seen at Hadley Junction. Unfortunately, no.1663 also disgraced itself, becoming derailed at the crossing gates at Oakengates and requiring the Shrewsbury breakdown train hauled by a G2 0-8-0 to visit the line and crane the pannier tank back on to the tracks.

Once the passenger trains had ceased, the line was worked as 'One Engine in Steam' and the locomotive crew would be responsible for operating the crossing gates at Oakengates. The 'One Engine in Steam' principle made shunting easier, as the train could be left on the running line without fear of blocking any other workings.

A G2 0-8-0 with a breakdown crane on its way to re-rail a loco that has come off the rails near Oakengates.
A.J.B. DODD

The sidings at Hadley Junction remained in use until the mid-1960s for Sankeys traffic and later for the storage of wagons.

The responsibility for motive power passed from the LMS to the Western Region in 1950 and this changed the type of engines seen on the branch, with more ex-GWR locomotives appearing. The motive power seen on the branch was pretty consistent, with the same old locomotives seen daily. As one of the freight trains down to Coalport was the responsibility of Shrewsbury shed, with the train originating at Coton Hill Yard and returning there in the evening, some of Shrewsbury shed's elderly ex-MR 3F 0-6-0 locomotives, such as no.43822, were seen, as well as some of Shrewsbury's ex-LNWR G2 0-8-0s, such as no.49276, and 94XX pannier tanks such as nos 8449, 9470 and 9472, the latter being quite distinctive as part of the smoke-box number plate was missing.

Burton shed's 0-6-0s would also be seen on the 'mid-morning' goods, although this service actually arrived in the early afternoon; 3F 0-6-0s examples seen were nos 43709 and 43809 and 4F 0-6-0s were nos 43948, 43976, 44124 and 44434. Presumably these locomotives had worked into Shrewsbury and been used on the Coalport trips. Another 3F, no.43652, was also seen at Oakengates, but the shed allocation is not known to the author.

As Shrewsbury was responsible for the motive power on the pick-up freight, every now and again a locomotive not usually seen would appear and Black Five no.45143 was seen on the line with the morning goods. In 1957, an ex-works condition locomotive from Bath Green Park, no.44917, appeared, no doubt having worked to Shrewsbury on a running-in turn from Crewe works and then purloined by Shrewsbury shed for the goods to Coalport.

Occasionally an excursion would be seen on the line and in the mid-1950s an ex-LNWR G2 0-8-0 was used on an eight-coach train. Another excursion train was seen with ten coaches, with a Crab 2-6-0 at its head on the outbound train, but a G2 for the return working. In 1956, two excursion trains were run to the North Wales coast, both of which were hauled by Black Five 4-6-0s and with one of them not stopping at Oakengates, one of the few occasions that a passenger train worked non-stop through the station.

Richard Derry, who visited his grandfather on holidays at Oakengates in the 1950s and observed the branch keenly, spotted a most unusual locomotive when he saw an ex-GWR 2-8-0 tender engine on a special freight for the Lilleshall Company; sadly, the number was not recorded.

On 23 April 1955, the Stephenson Locomotive Society ran a Special down the branch, hauled by one of the last Dean Goods 0-6-0s, no.2516. On 2 September 1959, the Stephenson Locomotive Society ran another Special, this time a Swindon three-car DMU.

Perhaps the most unusual working was the Western Region Gauging Train, which consisted of an elderly wooden-bodied coach with a clerestory roof acting as an Inspection Saloon, plus a wagon and brake van. This was seen at the sidings for the Lilleshall Company with a Wellington BR Standard Class 3 2-6-2 tank, no.82031. Ivatt Class 2 2-6-0 no.46524 of Shrewsbury shed was seen on the demolition train in November 1964.

CHAPTER 6

The Much Wenlock Branch

The line to Much Wenlock and beyond to Craven Arms was opened in stages between 1857 and 1862 as far as Much Wenlock, but it was 1867 before a connection was made to reach Craven Arms. As much of the line is outside the boundary for Telford, this book will only cover in photographs and text as far as Buildwas Junction.

The Much Wenlock Branch Line

Upon leaving the bay platforms at Wellington, the passenger trains would travel on the main line towards Oakengates and Wolverhampton. Soon after leaving Wellington, Stafford Junction was passed on the left and immediately after passing the junction sidings on the left further sidings served Haybridge Iron Company. The works became Haybridge Steel Company in 1945 and the sidings were closed on 14 June 1969. Like a number of locations in the area, Haybridge Iron Company also had a connection to the LNWR line to Stafford, as the works were located in the 'V' of the LNWR line to Stafford and the Great Western to Wolverhampton.

A signal box controlled the access into Haybridge Iron Company, but this was removed in 1932 and replaced by a ground frame. Prior to the closure of the signal box it was operated by a signal man from Ketley, who would walk to the box on the three days a week that a service called at the ironworks. After the signal box was removed, the ground frame was operated by the guard after it had been unlocked by

the signalman at Wellington no.1, who could see the sidings from his box.

After passing Haybridge Iron Company, Ketley Junction was reached, which turned south of the main line and had two sidings parallel with the branch line. The junction was controlled by a signal box, which closed on 10 September 1967. The sidings alongside the branch were removed in May 1963.

After leaving the junction, next came a set of sidings serving the Wrekin Foundry. This had originally been James Clay's works opened in 1924 to produce agricultural machinery. Between 1942 and 1946, the site was taken over by the Admiralty, but for what purpose is unknown to the author. From 1947 it was owned by Aga Heat for the making of Aga stoves.

After passing the sidings for the Wrekin Foundry, Ketley station was reached, with a set of crossing gates at the platform end that crossed the busy A5 trunk road from London to Holyhead.

Ketley Station

The station originally had two ground frames and a signal box (built in 1893 and rebuilt in 1924), but these were replaced by the signal box in 1926. In 1893–4, the station was improved with a new signal box and platform extensions. There was a single platform with a two-storey station building and a lengthy goods loop that would hold forty-two wagons. At the end of the platform facing

The level crossing and signal box at Ketley station in September 1964.
KIDDERMINSTER RAILWAY MUSEUM

trains from Wellington there was a level crossing, meaning that northbound trains prevented the gates being opened until the train had departed. At the south of the goods loop there was a head shunt with a connection into Sinclair Ironworks.

Whilst Ketley had no goods yard, there was extensive traffic in and out of the two ironworks, with inbound traffic including: pig iron from Holwell Junction and Kettering; limestone from Wirksworth; scrap iron from Shropshire, Cheshire, North Wales and Lancashire; sand from Shifnal;

and coke from various sources. The outbound traffic was drainpipes, manhole covers and other finished products. The goods office for Ketley was not in the station but was situated inside Sinclair's Ironworks, as this was the destination for most of the traffic in and out. The volume of traffic in and out of the Sinclair Foundry was such that the Great Western in 1921 asked the foundry to increase its siding capacity, as the GW engine was spending so much time shunting; this does not appear to have been heeded.

Passengers wait at Ketley station as a DMU from Wellington to Much Wenlock approaches. At least the single railcar will not be overwhelmed with passengers. A.J.B. DODD

The very basic facilities can be seen here at Ketley Town Halt, opened in 1936. The siding on the left is the head shunt for the Sinclair Ironworks, which can be seen in the distance.
D. CLARKE

Ketley Town Halt

This was opened on 6 March 1936 as part of Great Western's attempts to compete with the ever increasing local bus services. The long head shunt from the Sinclair Ironworks at Ketley terminated by the wooden platform.

New Dale Halt

This was opened on 29 January 1934. The station consisted of a basic single wooden platform.

Lawley Bank Station

Lawley Bank station was next down the line and again was a single platform with a small signal box at the platform end adjacent to the crossing gates. There were no goods facilities at the station and the platforms had been extended by 1902.

After leaving Lawley Bank, the gradient rose to 1 in 45, then the line passed through Horsehay Tunnel, over which the Dawley to Wellington Road travelled.

Lawley Bank station in 1961 facing towards Wellington and showing the covered ground at the end of the platform. R.G. NELSON

Horsehay and Dawley Station

The next station on the line had a single platform with a small signal box that had been installed in 1893. In the 1930s, there were four staff at the station.

Adjacent to the station was the Horsehay Ironworks. In addition to the Ironworks sidings, there were other sidings. The Horsehay Company had two small 0-4-0 shunting locomotives, but these were both scrapped in 1953/4 and any required shunting was carried out either by a BR locomotive or by a road tractor. By 1901, the Horsehay Company site was extensive with its large high buildings (needed to build bridge structures, blast furnace ladles and cranes) commanding the countryside. The Horsehay works specialized in the production of bridge girders and the site had a large travelling crane for loading and unloading steel and finished products. The Horsehay Company had its own private owner mineral wagons that could be seen on the national rail network.

An open-cast coal mine was opened in 1942 and this supplied slack coal to Buildwas Power Station, with one train a day leaving the site.

During World War II, Horsehay manufactured landing craft, radar antennae and radar discs. The very large assembly shop was built in about 1950, to assemble the steelwork's cranes. Until this time, everything was assembled outdoors; ice and snow was brushed off to get to work.

The company was taken over in the early 1960s by Joseph Adamson and thereafter a number of different owners before its final purchaser, Norcros Group. During this era, the Horsehay works supplied products to the steel and railway industries, particularly heavy lifting cranes to customers all around the globe.

Horsehay and Dawley station on 25 June 1961 showing the nine-lever signal box. There was an extensive goods yard with ten sidings serving the large Horsehay Company works, which is behind the photographer. R.G. NELSON

A view of Horsehay and Dawley with the sidings for the Horsehay Company in the distance and with an LMS wagon just visible in the upper left. The rising gradient through the station is highlighted by the sidings being on the level. D. CLARKE

The last riveted bridge structure, which was a crane structure for R.T.B. (Llanwern Steelworks), was assembled in 1971. The works finally closed in 1984 and the imposing buildings were demolished. The site is now part of the Telford Steam Railway.

Doseley Halt

Doseley Halt was the next station on the line. It was opened on 1 December 1932 and again was a simple one-platform station with no passenger accommodation, but with a level crossing next to the small covered ground frame. After leaving Doseley Halt, the line passed Dawley Parva Level Crossing.

Originally there had been sidings serving the former Lightmoor Furnaces, built in 1858, but these closed in 1883 and the sidings were removed. There was a ground frame to control access into these sidings and also to work the crossing gates for the road between Little Dawley and Lightmoor.

The line then continued towards Lightmoor Junction, where the line from Madeley Junction came in from the left. Before reaching Lightmoor Junction, the traces of various plateways to Dawley Parva Colliery could be seen, but is not clear whether these made a connection with the standard gauge line.

Lightmoor and Lightmoor junction

This area was once a hive of industry, with the Lightmoor Brick and Tileworks and Lightmoor Furnaces adjacent to the junction. The tileworks of Shutfield Brick and Tileworks as well as the Cherry Tree Hill Brick and Tileworks were also located there and were connected to the main line by a plateway, or mineral railway, which ran into the back of the goods yard to enable trans-shipment of materials and goods out. In the 1880s, Lightmoor Colliery was also connected to the junction by a mineral line, but by 1902 this had been closed. Lightmoor Ironworks was opened in 1775 and continued until 1883, when the site became derelict. The last horse-drawn plateway was between Lightmoor Brick and

The Horsehay Steam Trust operates from the yard at Horsehay station and in 1980 ex-GWR 5619 is seen next to the North British shunter, which once worked at Sankey, Hadley. In the background can be seen the large Horsehay buildings, now demolished. D. CLARKE

Doseley Halt between Horsehay and Lightmoor was opened in 1932 in response to increased competition from buses, hence the modest (and therefore cheap) station facilities. The view is looking towards Wellington. D. CLARKE

Lightmoor Junction on 21 June 1962, with the line from Madeley Junction coming in from the left. The sidings on the far right used to serve the Lightmoor Brickworks and Lightmoor Ironworks; these are covered by trees.
KIDDERMINSTER RAILWAY MUSEUM

Tileworks and the foundry at Coalbrookdale; this did not close until October 1932.

The original wooden signal box with its twenty-five levers was opened around 1875 and was on the Madeley branch immediately after the junction, but this was demolished in 1951. It was replaced by a brick and concrete box (with a flat concrete roof), which was located at the end of Lightmoor platform. The signal box continued to be in use even after the line from Ketley closed, but in 2006, when changes were made to the signalling arrangements and Lightmoor Junction box closed, control was passed to Madeley Junction.

On the opposite side of the junction were four sidings, one of which served a wooden goods shed along with a weighbridge and weighing machine house. In the 1920s, this goods shed was used by the Coalbrookdale Company for the storage of tiles before shipment out by rail. Ballast sidings were added on the Wellington line just past the junction in 1900, but these had been removed by 1927. Given the activities elsewhere in the area, the author suspects that these ballast sidings were added to allow the slag from the closed Lightmoor Ironworks to be used as ballast elsewhere on the GWR system.

Lightmoor Junction is seen in 1963 with the 1951-built signal box on the left (replacing a box previously on the Madeley line). The line ahead is to Horsehay and on to Wellington and the line to the right is to Madeley Junction. The photographer is standing on Lightmoor station.
P.J. GARLAND

Adjacent to Lightmoor Junction was the station opened in 1907 and known as Lightmoor Platform, later shortened to Lightmoor. It displays its GWR pagoda-style station building. The downhill gradient can be seen in the distance in this 1963 photograph. P.J. GARLAND

The modest station was opened on 12 August 1907 after a request was made by Madeley District Council to the GWR to open a station there. It was originally called Lightmoor Platform, before reverting to just Lightmoor. The platforms were wooden and the station buildings were in the typical rural GWR pagoda style, being cheaply made from corrugated iron sheets. The booking office was below the platforms at road level. Neither gas nor electric lighting was provided at the station. The station was past the junction in the direction of Coalbrookdale.

Green Bank Halt

Before Coalbrookdale was reached, Green Bank Halt was another of the simple single-platform stations and was opened on 12 March 1934.

Leaving Green Bank, the falling gradient of 1 in 50 led to the crossing of Coalbrookdale Viaduct,

consisting of twenty-six curved arches, then passing over the Upper Furnace pool and part of the Coalbrookdale Company's works before entering Coalbrookdale station.

Coalbrookdale Station

Coalbrookdale was a substantial station with two platforms and stone-built station buildings. A signal box was built in 1863 and when the line was improved in the 1890s a new signal box was erected with fifteen levers, but this was closed in 1955 and two ground frames replaced it, one at either end of the platforms. These were then closed in 1965 and 1967. The station had two goods sidings at the Buildwas end of the station, but these were taken out of use in 1965.

There were interchange sidings with the Coalbrookdale Company, which generated a large

This view of the viaduct at Coalbrookdale shows a Much Wenlock train with one of the GWR steam railcars introduced in 1906. However, their use on these services was short-lived, as they struggled on the gradients. On market days, in order to cater for additional passengers a trailing car was added, giving further problems. The railcars were taken away in 1907. D. CLARKE

A general view of Coalbrookdale with the sidings to the Coalbrookdale works on the right full of wagons. D. CLARKE

Another view of Coalbrookdale with one of the many plateways that crossed the landscape even after the 'proper railways' had arrived. In the background is Holy Trinity Church built in 1854 and to the right of the church is Coalbrookdale Company's Library and Scientific Institute built in 1859. D. CLARKE

amount of freight traffic averaging 25,000 tons per year and this kept five staff occupied. The Coalbrookdale Company had its own shunting locomotives to take wagons from the GW in and out of the works. The Coalbrookdale Company built two 0-4-0 saddle tanks in 1865 for this work, no.5 and no.6; no.5 was sold in 1932 and has subsequently been preserved. No.6 was rebuilt by Sentinel of Shrewsbury, with a vertical boiler and the chassis of this is similarly preserved. In 1943, a Peckett 0-4-0 was purchased. This locomotive is also now preserved. Rail traffic in and out of the Coalbrookdale works ceased in 1960 and after the closure of the passenger services on the line one of the station buildings remained well into the 1980s.

Buildwas Station

This was again a substantial station with two sets of platforms, one for the Wellington to Much Wenlock line and a separate set at a lower level for the Shrewsbury to Kidderminster line. To allow passengers to change trains at the station there were wooden steps connecting the upper and lower platforms. The lower platforms had the main station buildings, although the upper platform had a small waiting room.

A large water tower on a brick base was located on the west end of the branch platform. As it was a junction there were two signal boxes, Buildwas Junction and Buildwas Station Signal Box. In November 1923, a new signal box containing sixty-six levers was built, replacing the two former signal boxes. In December 1931, the new signal box was

Coalbrookdale no.5 built in 1865 waits at the top of the sidings leading from the GWR line down to the works. The engine was later sold but survived until 1959, when it was returned to Coalbrookdale for preservation. The primitive cab of a typical industrial loco can be seen.
J.A. PEDEN

extended to 113 levers in anticipation of the opening of the power station.

The sidings were extended with the opening in 1932 of the Buildwas Power Station and 300,000 tons of goods were booked through the station, mainly coal for the power station. The turntable situated in the yard was removed in 1936.

With the closure of the line to Much Wenlock and the line from Shrewsbury to Kidderminster, the site of Buildwas station was radically changed with the building of the B Power Station. Most of the existing trackwork was taken up in 1964 and the new 'merry-go-round' trackwork installed.

An ex-GWR home and distant signal at Coalbrookdale, facing Wellington and with the line to the right going down into the Coalbrookdale works. R. CARPENTER

Buildwas Junction facing Much Wenlock (the platform on the left) and on the right the Severn Valley line to Bridgnorth and Kidderminster in February 1962. P.J. GARLAND

Buildwas Junction facing Bridgnorth, showing the Severn Valley platforms to Bridgnorth and Kidderminster, with the Wellington to Much Wenlock platforms on a higher level to the left in February 1962. P.J. GARLAND

Buildwas Junction facing towards Coalbrookdale, showing the Much Wenlock platforms in February 1962. P.J. GARLAND

The station at Buildwas was an important junction, with trains from Shrewsbury down the Severn Valley to Bridgnorth and beyond, as well as trains to Much Wenlock and to Craven Arms. This shows the station name board with a space formerly filled with Craven Arms, but the line past Much Wenlock was closed to passengers in December 1951. P.J. GARLAND

Buildwas Junction was effectively two stations back to back and shown here is the line from Shrewsbury facing towards Bridgnorth, with the Wellington to Much Wenlock platforms at a slightly higher level to the right on 18 February 1962. P.J. GARLAND

Another view of the Severn Valley line platforms at Buildwas station, showing the relationship to the CEGB Power station in 1962.
P.J. GARLAND

With closure of Buildwas A station in the late 1970s, there was less need for the steam shunters, as the B station was on the 'merry-go-round' principle. Here, no.3 is seen shunting oil tanks for the A station in July 1976. G. CRYER

Buildwas (Ironbridge) Power Station

The Ironbridge Gorge was selected by the West Midlands Electricity Authority in 1927 for the building of a large superstation, because of the close proximity of the river for cooling water and rail lines for the delivery of coal. Construction of what was to be Ironbridge A started in 1929 and the station was officially opened on 13 October 1932, although full capacity was not realized until 1939 with the commissioning of extra boilers and generators giving a capacity of 200mW. The creation of the power station resulted in considerable changes to Buildwas Junction station, with additional sidings being provided on both the up and down sides and the signal box extended.

In 1975, more sidings were added for oil tanker wagons that could be worked into the A station. The A station continued to operate until 1980, when half of the station's capacity was shut down, followed by the remaining capacity in 1981. The A station was demolished in 1983.

The construction of the B station, which had been approved in 1962, commenced in 1963 and with the closure of all passenger services through Buildwas Junction station in July 1962, part of the land occupied by the railway station was used for building the new B power station. The revised layout for the sidings feeding the power station incorporated automatic hoppers, allowing the new-style 'merry-go-round' trains to be used with special hopper wagons that could be automatically discharged. The B station had a capacity of 1,000 mW from two 500mW generators. Power was fed into the National Grid in 1969 and full capacity was reached in February 1970.

Ironbridge no.1 was a Pecket build of 1933 and was delivered new to the power station and remained at the station until withdrawn in the 1970s with the running down of Ironbridge A station. The locomotive is preserved at the Foxfield Railway. D. CLARKE

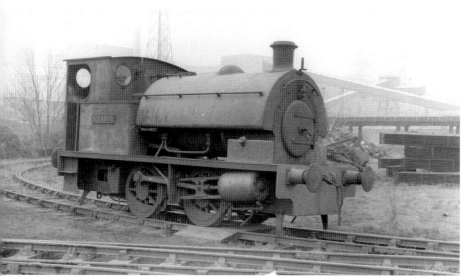

Buildwas Power Station had three steam shunters and here no.1 Anne, a Bagnall product of 1945, is seen out of use at the power station. It had arrived in 1964 and did little work before being withdrawn in 1967. D. CLARKE

Coal for both stations was worked in from Madeley Junction, with Granville Colliery supplying coal until its closure in 1979. Production ceased in May 1979 and the last consignment of coal left the pit in June 1979.

Motive power for the coal trains from Granville was supplied by a mixture of locomotives from Shrewsbury, usually an 8F 2-8-0, and Wellington, which would supply a 0-6-0 pannier tank for the shorter trains. In the late 1950s, ex-GW 2-6-0s were seen on these trains at Madeley Junction and Buildwas, but presumably they had picked up the coal trains at either Wellington or Hollinswood. With the closure of Wellington shed and the run-down at

Shrewsbury, Oxley shed (Wolverhampton) became responsible for the motive power and 8F 2-8-0s nos 48680 and 48724 were both observed on coal trains. BR Standard Class 4 4-6-0s (including no.75024), BR Standard Class 4 2-6-0s (including no.76039) and ex-GWR Manor 4-6-0s (such as no.7821) were all also observed on the workings. In addition, ex-GW 0-6-2 tank no.5606 of Tysley shed was seen on these workings. One of Oxley shed's 2-8-2 tanks was seen banking the heavy oil trains through Coalbrookdale in the mid-1950s.

Between 3,000 and 6,000 tons of coal were delivered every day, but after the closure of Granville Colliery coal came from various sources, one regular working being a coal train from Silverdale Colliery in Stoke. Because of emission regulations and a desire to reduce emissions at the station, three trains a day ran from Liverpool Docks with biomass chips (wood chips, all the way from America!). This was mixed 20 per cent with coal to reduce emissions. The power station was slated for closure in 2015.

To shunt the wagons in and out of the A station, several steam locomotives were used at various times: no.1, a Peckett build of 1933; no.2, a Peckett

of 1936; and no.3, another Peckett of 1940. No.2 was transferred away in 1951 to another power station and in 1964 no.1 *Anne*, a William Bagnall build of 1945, arrived, but did little work except filling in when one of the other two locomotives was not available. With the closure of the A station and with the B station using 'merry-go-round' hoppers, there was little or no further use for the shunters and in 1980 the two remaining locomotives left. No.1 went to the Foxfield Railway and no.3 went to the Horsehay Trust. Peckett no.2 is also preserved.

On 29 September 1986, diesel Class 58 no.58042 was named *Ironbridge Power Station* as this class of freight locomotives was used on the 'merry-go-round' hopper trains. The name was subsequently transferred to 58005 on 12 May 1996.

Operating the Line

At the turn of the century, Wolverhampton-built 0-6-0 saddle tanks worked the Wenlock trains. In May 1906, steam railcars were tried on the line, but the gradients proved too much, particularly on market days when an additional coach was attached, which made getting away from stations

An ex-GWR railcar known as a 'Flying Banana' at Buildwas on a Severn Valley working. These single railcars supplemented the two-coach steam workings between Shrewsbury and Kidderminster. A.J.B. DODD

Buildwas Junction in May 1961, with a train from Wellington to Much Wenlock entering the station. Loaded coal wagons for the power station can be seen on the right, with the power station off camera to the left. The sizeable ex-GWR signal box can also be seen. R.G. NELSON

somewhat problematic. The railcars were replaced later in 1906 by 2-4-0 tanks. In later years, 44XX 2-6-2 tanks were used. However, the GWR had not given up on railcars and in 1937 the diesel railcars known as 'Flying Bananas' were tried, but yet again the gradients proved too much and the service reverted once more to steam power.

In 1938, a petrol depot was built on the site of former quarry sidings known as Bradley Sidings near to Farley Halt on the line from Buildwas to Much Wenlock. During World War II, this generated much additional traffic passing through to Buildwas. The type of motive power used on these trains was completely different to that normally seen, including 4-6-0 Halls, Granges and Manors as well as 28XX 2-8-0s and 72XX 2-8-2 tanks. The loads were heavy, with twenty-five tank wagons not being unusual, but the steep gradients would sometimes catch out drivers who were not familiar with the route, particularly from Farley to Buildwas. The empty petrol trains were worked

in from Shrewsbury to Buildwas via the Severn Valley line, but it is not known to the author if all the loaded trains worked back to Shrewsbury from Buildwas, or if some went out via Buildwas and Madeley Court to Madeley Junction. The sidings for the petrol depot were taken out of use in 1948, though it seems likely there had been little or no traffic once the war finished in 1945. The location was determined by its distance from the coast and German bombing.

The two ironworks at Ketley, Wrekin Foundry and Sinclair Ironworks, particularly the latter, generated much traffic, with wagonloads from many parts of the country coming in and finished products going out. In the 1920s and 1930s, traffic for the ironworks would come in on the 11.25am freight from Wellington, which would run through to Much Wenlock, but as the load for a pannier tank was twelve mineral wagons (due to the gradient from the junction), a banker would assist into the goods loop. Once the train arrived at Ketley, the banker

One of Wellington's pannier tanks waits at Ketley with a service from Much Wenlock. The old colliery spoil tip to the right was a feature across the area until the New Town cleared all these away. Sinclair Ironworks' roof can be seen in the right background. A.J.B. DODD

Coalbrookdale station on 25 July 1959, with 9630 on the 7.05am from Much Wenlock to Wellington. The line curving away to the left is the siding down to the Coalbrookdale works. KIDDERMINSTER RAILWAY MUSEUM

would return to Wellington. Outward-bound traffic from Ketley would be cleared by the 4.50pm freight from Horsehay, which had left Wellington at 3.00pm and often ran engine and brake van from Ketley to Horsehay (having dropped off wagons at Ketley).

Horsehay had a small yard dealing with the usual coal traffic and a small goods shed. There was also a wharf where slack for the newly opened Buildwas Power Station was loaded, as well as stone ballast. Outbound traffic included sewer pipes from the Doseley Pipe Company.

Adjacent to the station there was a large slag heap, which had been deposited by the Coalbrookdale Company's furnaces between 1755 and 1886. Up to 1939, this heap was slowly reduced, as the slag was used as ballast by the GWR for sidings and yards; every week a train of this ballast would leave Horsehay for some point on the Great Western. There

was also a connection into the Horsehay Company, which made bridge girders and other large fabricated steel structures. Inbound traffic included steel plate for this company. In the 1930s 30,000 tons of goods were booked through the station, about half of which consisted of mineral wagonloads.

After the closure of the line, the rail connection remained into the works and trains worked in and out as required. The trains reversed at the station and went down the line to Lightmoor Junction, where the train would again reverse and proceed to Madeley Junction. When trains were run, two locomotives were provided due to the steep descent of 1 in 40 down to Lightmoor Junction. The connection remained into the Horsehay works site until the 1980s. Since the works had lost its rail link to the main line, many of these huge engineered products had to be transported to their destinations by

41201 of Wellington shed is seen on the viaduct at Coalbrookdale on 9 June 1962 with a Much Wenlock train a month before the service ceased. M. MENSING

road. Indeed, some of the longest and heaviest engineered products that ever travelled on British roads set out on their journeys from the little village of Horsehay in Shropshire.

The Railway Magazine of November 1971 gave a description by the late Geoffrey Bannister of one of the special trains that ran on 2 September 1971 with a single load of an overhead crane destined for Motherwell. The empty wagons, usually special low-loader wagons such as Macaws, would be delivered two or three days before the move. The works would then load and chain down the load. This loading and chaining down would take place within the site and in the absence of a proper railway shunter, the load would be pulled out of the works, across the road and into the goods yard. Here, the motive power, usually a Bescot-allocated Class 24 (in this case D5137 in green

with full yellow ends) with a brake van, would be waiting, along with a second locomotive, usually a Class 08 diesel 0-6-0 shunter from Wellington (in the example, no.3397, also with a brake van). After some shunting, the train was ready to depart, with both locomotives at the front and a brake van at either end. After reversing at Lightmoor Junction, the 08 remained at Lightmoor, while the Class 24 took the train to Madeley Junction, where another reversal took place. Having completed its task, the Class 24 departed back to Bescot and the 08 shunter, having followed from Lightmoor, was then coupled on to the front of the train to take it to Wellington. From there, another main-line locomotive would take the load onwards to Motherwell. Another working on 30 April 1979 had another Class 25, no.25009, and a 0-6-0 diesel shunter, no.08019, take a single load out of the works.

Wellington shed's 2-6-2 tank no.4178 is seen at Buildwas on the last day of services to Much Wenlock, hence the three well-filled coaches. Previously, the two coaches normally used would have been sparsely occupied. The engine has been especially cleaned by the shed staff at Wellington. D. CLARKE

A train from Much Wenlock passes the Sinclair Foundry approaching Ketley station on 21 June 1962. KIDDERMINSTER RAILWAY MUSEUM

CHAPTER 7

The Severn Valley Route – Buildwas to Coalport (GWR)

Within the boundary of Telford there were a number of stations situated on the Shrewsbury to Kidderminster line that need inclusion in this book.

The Severn Valley line was built between 1858 and 1862 and was formally absorbed by the Great Western Railway in 1870. The railway linked Shrewsbury in the north with Buildwas, Bridgnorth, Bewdley and Kidderminster, where it joined the main line from Birmingham to Worcester via Stourbridge.

The Buildwas to Coalport (GWR) Line

The line left the main station at Shrewsbury from a bay platform, diverged from the line to Hereford at Abbey Foregate and crossed through farming country at Berrington and Cressage, before arriving at Buildwas. Buildwas has already been described with its two sets of platforms, one for the Wellington to Much Wenlock trains, and a separate set of platforms for the Severn Valley line.

Ironbridge and Broseley Station

After leaving Buildwas, the first station on the line was Ironbridge and Broseley, where the station overlooked the river gorge and the Ironbridge. The station had a signal box, which opened in 1870, and a wooden goods shed. It was approached by a single line that opened out to two tracks within the station, allowing two platforms and also for trains

to pass. There were a number of sidings on both the up and down side before the line became a single line again.

The signal box was closed in 1956 and the top half removed to make a store room. The station was equipped with a metal footbridge and like many of the stations there was a level crossing at the platform ends. At the south end of the station, there was a connection into the Coalport Brick and Tileworks.

Before Jackfield Halt was reached, there were sidings at Jackfield that serviced a number of tile-works.

Jackfield Halt

This opened in December 1934, but was closed in March 1954 due to the danger of the station slipping into the River Severn. The station was replaced by a similar single wooden platform further down the line past the Maws Sidings that was opened in March 1954.

Coalport and the GW station also overlooked the competition, with the ex-LNWR line to Coalport visible on the opposite bank as well.

Maws Sidings

The sidings served Maw and Company (also known as the Benthal Encaustic Tileworks), which had moved onto the site in 1883. At the height of the boom in tiles the company was producing over 20 million tiles per year. The site covered over 5 acres

BENTHALL BANK FROM IRONBRIDGE.

A view of Ironbridge and Broseley station in the early years of the twentieth century. The steep road in the background is Bentham Bank and the Ironbridge can be seen on the far right. D. CLARKE

Ironbridge and Broseley station in the early years of the twentieth century with an elderly GWR locomotive on a passenger service of six-wheeled coaches. D. CLARKE

(2 hectares) and at the end of the century was the largest tileworks in the world.

In the decades after World War II, the company gradually declined and the works finally closed in January 1970. In the mid-1970s, two-thirds of the works was demolished, but the remainder of the site has been preserved, with the buildings split into small business units and flats, as well as a craft centre.

Coalport (GWR)

The single line again branched out into two platforms, with extensive station buildings and a brick-built waiting room on the other side. On the south side of the station there were sidings and a connection into Exley Tileworks. These tileworks were taken over by the Ministry of Munitions in 1917 for the storage of ammunition. Following World War I, the site became Coalport Refectories,

A BR single railcar on a Kidderminster to Shrewsbury train at Jackfield Halt in August 1963. F.W. SHUTTLEWORTH

Coalport GW station is seen here on 7 July 1963 looking towards Bridgnorth with some of the sidings showing little use. R. CARPENTER

Coalport station seen on 25 May 1961 facing towards Bridgnorth. R.G. NELSON

which closed in 1954 and the sidings connecting it to the station were removed in 1957. The signal box was adjacent to the sidings.

Operating the Line

The passenger trains were Shrewsbury to Bridgnorth or Shrewsbury to Kidderminster and in the 1920s the line, like the Wellington to Crewe services, was the last haunt of elderly Great Western tank and tender engines. So as an example in 1915 a Kidderminster to Shrewsbury freight was hauled by a double-framed 0-6-0,

no.946 of Class 927. These elderly 0-6-0 tender engines were also seen on passenger trains. Given the small size of many of the stations on the line, the passenger service was modest, with two coaches sufficing. Freight traffic was also light, with only the coal traffic from Alveley being of any consequence.

In the 1950s, there was a 5.30pm departure from Shrewsbury to Birmingham Snow Hill via the Severn Valley line and Kidderminster's 41XX 2-6-2 tanks could be seen on this service. In 1954, one of Kidderminster's 45XX 2-6-2 tanks, no.4567, was noted on the service.

Ex-GWR 2-6-2 tank no.5147 is seen entering Coalport with a passenger train down the Severn Valley line. D. CLARKE

A passenger train pulled by 2-6-2 tank no.5518 is seen at Coalport GWR on the Severn Valley line on 23 April 1957. M. HALE

41203 from Shrewsbury shed enters Ironbridge and Broseley in 1962 with a Shrewsbury to Kidderminster train. The former signal box to the right of the engine has now been turned into a storeroom. R. CARPENTER

A Great Western double-framed 0-6-0 at Arley on a Kidderminster to Shrewsbury freight in 1915. Just outside the Telford boundary, but it shows the type of locomotive and freight that would be seen at Buildwas and on the Severn Valley line.
BURNHAM COLLECTION

BR Standard Class 3 2-6-2 tank no.82009 on a service to Shrewsbury at Coalport (GW) station. 82009 was a Shrewsbury engine for three months in 1959, before moving to Wellington.
A.J.B. DODD

In BR days, ex-GW 2-6-2 tanks, both of the small-wheeled 55XX and the larger-wheeled 51XX types, would be seen on passenger services. Sometimes 57XX pannier tanks were also seen on passenger trains, with some of Worcester's allocation noted. The large-wheeled 2-6-2 tanks, such as no.5147 and no.5153, could be seen hauling freight trains. As Shrewsbury was responsible for much of the motive power at this time, its ex-LMS Ivatt 2-6-2 tanks such as no.41203 and also the BR Class 4 2-6-4 tanks 80XXX were seen after they arrived at Shrewsbury shed in 1962, no.80100 being noted on October 1962 and no.80102 on the last day of service in 1963.

Ex-GWR single railcars were also used on services from Shrewsbury to Bridgnorth or the Shrewsbury to Hartelbury from 1942, with W20W and W5W being seen on these services as the small number of passengers could easily be accommodated by a single coach. These GW railcars were replaced by BR-built single DMUs for the last six months of services in 1963. The steam services generally were of two coaches. Some of Shrewsbury's BR Standard Class 3 2-6-2 tanks were also seen on the passenger services, with no.82009 seen in 1959. Some of the passenger trains from Shrewsbury would terminate at Bridgnorth.

Ex-GWR 2-6-2 tank 4129 shunts at Ironbridge and Broseley station with the famous Ironbridge to the right. The freight train is blocking the line whilst the shunting is taking place. D. CLARKE

2-6-2 tank 5153 seen at Ironbridge and Broseley with a coal train heading towards Buildwas, probably originating from the colliery at Alveley. LENS OF SUTTON

Alveley Colliery was located further down the line south of Bridgnorth near to Hampton Loade and the majority of its coal was shipped out down to Kidderminster, but some traffic went north to Buildwas Power Station or to Shrewsbury. The 1960 *Working Time Table* lists two weekday freights on the route, the 12.50am coal empties from Buildwas to Alveley Sidings, and the 11.25am Shrewsbury (Coton Hill) to Kidderminster. Both of these trains were to be run as required.

Unsurprisingly, the services on the Severn Valley line finished in September 1963 and in fact termination had been announced before the Beeching Plan was published. Ivatt Class 2 41207 of Shrewsbury was seen on one of the last passenger trains, the 9.50am from Shrewsbury.

CHAPTER 8

The Lilleshall Company

The Lilleshall Company was the colossus that strode over East Shropshire, becoming the largest employer in the region by utilizing the local iron, coal and limestone reserves to produce iron and steel, manufacture complex engineering products and produce bricks, tiles and sanitary ware. The company also delivered coal all over the UK.

The Lilleshall Company was founded by the Leveson-Gower family, who owned large estates in Shropshire dating back to 1539. The second Earl Gower was looking to make best use of his estate and the minerals beneath them, but because he lacked knowledge in industrial matters, in 1764 he formed a partnership with the Gilbert Brothers. This partnership lasted until 1802 and during this period coal, limestone and iron deposits were developed and the Donnington Wood Canal was opened in 1768.

The Lilleshall Company was founded on 24 June 1802 when new partners joined and not only bought in new capital, but also mines and ironworks at Snedshill, Wrockwardine Wood and Donnington Wood. Subsequently, further partners joined, bringing in additional ironworks. In 1862, the company became a limited liability company with the name revised to the Lilleshall Company Limited in 1888.

Over the years, the company had a number of collieries, brickworks, furnaces, coke ovens, steelworks, engineering works, concrete works and an asphalt distillation plant. The picture, however, was constantly changing, with brickworks, coke ovens, fireclay mines, coal mines and ironworks opening

The Lilleshall Company built a number of locomotives, both for themselves and for other customers. This shows the builder's plate attached to one of its locomotives, no.2 built in 1886 for use at Priors Lee. D. CLARKE

One of the Lilleshall-built locos, no.2, is seen in 1933 in what looks like New Yard. D. CLARKE

and closing. By the 1930s, as well as the working assets, the area was littered with abandoned mines and derelict buildings, ironworks and foundries.

To move the limestone, coal and ironstone to the furnaces the company invested in the building of a number of canals and some horse-drawn tramways and plateways. In the 1840s, the arrival of the main-line railways through Wellington from Wolverhampton, Shrewsbury and Stafford effectively bounded the company's operations, in the north at Donnington and in the south at Hollinswood. At both locations the company could receive any raw materials and also ship out coal and finished goods.

The technology of the railways could also improve the company's internal logistics, so in the 1850s it began building its own standard-gauge railway, linking the majority of the company's sites with interchanges to the main-line railways at Donnington (LNWR), Hollinswood (GWR) and the Coalport branch (LNWR). The opening of New Yard

Engineering works in 1861 also provided the perfect location for the company's locomotive shed and repair facilities for both wagons and locomotives. At its peak, the Lilleshall Company had 26 miles (42km) of track to serve its various businesses. The interchange with the GWR at Hollinswood had extensive sidings, as the company imported its iron ore for the Priors Lee furnaces as well as coke from South Wales. The adjacent site of Snedshill had sidings coming off the LNWR Coalport branch (and also an access into Priors Lee) and the company had sidings at Donnington on the LNWR Stafford line for its coal from Granville and for the Lodge Furnaces.

The New Yard Engineering works gave the Lilleshall Company a modern engineering facility and the site produced blast furnace pumping engines, water pumping engines, winding machinery and steam hammers for external customers, as well as producing items for its own sites. The company, having built its own railway system and

THE LILLESHALL IRON & STEEL COMPANY LIMITED'S
BLAST FURNACES AND ROLLING MILLS.

An aerial view of the Priors Lee complex of the Lilleshall Company, with the steelworks centre left and the slagworks bottom right. One of the company's locomotives can be seen moving past the slagworks. IRONBRIDGE GORGE MUSEUM TRUST

having a modern engineering facility, found it was only a small step to building locomotives both for itself and for sale. The first locomotive to be built by the company was completed in 1862, a small 0-4-0 tank engine. New Yard continued spasmodically to build locomotives and tried to get into the market of supplying main-line locomotives to the smaller railway companies, but this breakthrough never happened as the company realized it could not compete against the larger-volume manufacturers. The company continued to build locomotives until the 1880s, with the last locomotive being completed in 1901. Because not all the locomotive build records have survived, the exact number is not clear, but is thought to be around fifty-two, with three further locomotives possibly built by the company.

The recession of the 1930s led to the closure of New Yard in 1931. However, the buildings

were reopened in the 1940s when the Lilleshall Company was awarded contracts for military work, with the New Yard buildings being used for the production of alloy steel armour-piercing shells. The Snedshill brickworks were used for heat treating of the metal. Other parts of New Yard were used for the production of military packaging and another contract was given for making shell caps, as well as reinforced rivets for use in armoured vehicles.

The Lilleshall Company had two sets of blast furnaces, one at Old Lodge Furnace built in 1824 (and closed in 1888), and the Priors Lee Furnaces, which became the main site for iron and steel production. The blast furnaces at Priors Lee were supplemented by some Bessemer convertors in the 1880s, allowing the company to be a steel maker and the output from these convertors was used in the rolling mill inside the steelworks. An open

9794. **THE LILLESHALL COMPANY LIMITED'S ENGINEERING WORKS.**

An aerial view of the New Yard Engineering works of the Lilleshall Company. Here, the company produced locomotives as well as blowing engines for the steel industry. The locomotive sheds are on the top right. IRONBRIDGE GORGE MUSEUM TRUST

hearth furnace was later installed enabling scrap metal to be used. The integrated blast furnaces and steel making continued until 1922 when imports of cheaper steel led to the closure of the steel-making plant. During the war years the blast furnaces were used to produce basic iron for other steelworks and the rolling mills continued on war work. However, by 1959 the blast furnaces were worn out having been built in 1900 and the cost of replacement was prohibitive in a very competitive market. So in March 1959 the last working blast furnace was blown out so ending a long tradition of iron making in East Shropshire.

The company had a large number of mines for coal, fireclay and iron ore, with many pits being originally sunk for ironstone and fireclay, but when these reserves ran out they were often then sunk deeper for coal. Many of the smaller pits were not rail-connected, but had tramway connections

to either ironworks or canals. The larger collieries also suffered closures over the years, such as Meadow (closed in 1894), Waxhill (closed in 1900), Lawn (closed in 1906), Muxton Bridge (closed in 1912), Stafford (closed in 1928), Freehold (closed in 1928), The Cockshutts (closed in 1940) and Woodhouse (closed in 1940), so by the mid-1940s the two major collieries remaining owned by the company were Granville Colliery and Grange Colliery, which were later connected underground.

The Nationalization of the coal mining industry in 1947 meant that the last two remaining Lilleshall Company coal mines passed to the National Coal Board (NCB), along with some of the company's locomotives to provide some motive power.

The company not only used coal for its iron-making, but also sold it locally into the domestic market and had private sidings at some stations

The Lilleshall Company was more than capable of rebuilding either locomotives it had built, or the second-hand ones it acquired and here no.1, an ex-Taff Vale 0-6-2 tank, is under repair in the steelworks in 1952. The engine survived until 1958. F.W. SHUTTLEWORTH

such as Trench and Shifnal to supply local coal merchants. The company also had contracts to supply locomotive coal to the LNWR, the GWR, the Great Central Railway, the North Staffordshire Railway and Cambrian Railways.

With the opening of the Buildwas Power Station in 1932, Granville Colliery supplied it with coal and this continued when the mines passed into NCB ownership.

The company supplied a number of cast-iron bridge girders, with the bridge over the canal at Trench Sidings and the bridge over the main road in Oakengates being identified with the company's name cast in. The bridge over the canal at Trench has since been removed.

An aerial view of the Lilleshall Company works at Priors Lee showing the steelworks in the background and with the slag plant in the foreground. IRONBRIDGE GORGE MUSEUM TRUST

Working the Lilleshall Railway System

To work the system and move the tonnage of raw materials involved required a number of locomotives to be in operation at the same time. In the 1850s, this was four locomotives rising to eight in the 1850s, then rising again to nine in 1900. The peak was reached in 1920, when eleven locomotives were used. During World War II, an operational fleet of nine locomotives was used, but after the war the requirement declined so that when the railway system closed down in 1959 only three locomotives were in use.

The Nationalization of the coal mines in 1947 meant that some of the company's locomotive fleet was transferred to the NCB. By definition, the level of traffic on what was left of the company's

Lilleshall no.10, a Peckett build of 1901, shunts in 1947 with what looks like pit props. D. CLARKE

One of the locomotives purchased by the Lilleshall Company was this Barclay 0-6-0 saddle tank in 1914 as Lilleshall no.3. The locomotive was scrapped on site in 1933. D. CLARKE

The Lilleshall Company not only built its own locomotives, but as the workload increased beyond the capacity of its small locomotives bought second-hand ones such as no.5, an ex-Barry Railway of 1892, which became GWR 251 before being sold to the Lilleshall Company in July 1934. It was withdrawn in January 1957 and is seen here in 1954. F.W. SHUTTLEWORTH

system also reduced. In the early part of the twentieth century as the loads on the internal system increased, it became clear that the locomotives built by the company in the 1860s and 1870s were now on the small side, so the company bought in larger locomotives from various sources, including second-hand engines from the main-line companies as well as new shunters from companies such as Barclay's of Scotland.

So, for example, two large 0-6-2 tanks built for the Taff Vale Railway in 1895 were bought from the Great Western Railway in May 1932. They were in excellent condition with nearly new boilers. The fleet was further added to by the purchase of an ex-Barry Railway 0-6-2 tank, which arrived in July 1934.

To convey the various raw materials and finished goods the company had an extensive fleet of wagons both for internal use and also for conveying goods on the main line. A summary is shown in the table.

The Lilleshall Company's Fleet of Wagons

Date	Main Line Wagons	Internal Use Wagons
1915	235	660
1925	351	439
1935	295	436
1944	180	482

*One of the last two operational locomotives on the Lilleshall system was **Alberta**, seen here in 1958 just before the rail system was closed.* D. CLARKE

The Lilleshall Company not only had its own locomotive fleet, but also owned a substantial number of wagons, both for internal use and also wagons owned by the company for running on the main line. Seen here is one of its wagons used for bringing limestone (necessary in the blast furnaces) from quarries in mid-Wales to Shropshire. HMRS

To maintain the wagon fleet the company had its own sawmill and wagon repair facility (built in 1902) at New Yard. Prior to 1901, the wagon repair facility was also in New Yard, but the building was converted to the locomotive repair facility adjacent to the locomotive running shed. After Nationalization of the main-line railway companies in 1948, the main-line wagon fleet was taken over by the newly formed British Railways and the wagons could thereafter be seen anywhere in the country displaying their increasingly faded Lilleshall livery. When the local supplies of iron ore became depleted, the Lilleshall Company used iron ore from the Wolstanton Pit at Stoke-on-Trent, so that company's wagons would then be seen at Priors Lee.

The company's internal rail network traversed a number of roads requiring the use of crossing keepers, but for certain crossings the railway always had the right of way at crossings.

The company had two locomotive sheds, one at New Yard and also a smaller single-road shed capable of holding two or three locomotives at the Priors Lee Furnaces. By having two locomotive

Lilleshall Company no.11 was purchased new from the Scottish builder Andrew Barclay in 1916 and continued to work until withdrawn in 1959 and scrapped on site.

Lilleshall no.6 is seen at the steelworks site; it was built in 1869, rebuilt in 1923 and scrapped in 1950.

Lilleshall no.12 *was an ex-GW pannier tank (no.2794) purchased in October 1950.*

sheds there was a considerable reduction in light-engine running. Iron ore for smelting at Priors Lee came in through the Hollinswood interchange and the smaller four coupled engines worked in the furnace area moving coal, coke and ash, as well as finished pig iron. These small shunters would also take ladles of molten slag to the slag bank.

The company's larger engines would be used on the runs to either the interchange at Donnington or Oakengates (on the Coalport branch), or to Hollinswood, as they had greater braking capacity for the gradients on the line and would be pulling wagons full of outgoing shipments of coal, rolled steel, pig iron and the corresponding empties.

Granville Colliery

This was the Lilleshall Company's largest coal mine and its products were of sufficient quality to be supplied to main-line railway companies (such as the LNWR, Cambrian Railways and so on), as well as domestic customers. From 1932, it supplied coal for Buildwas Power Station.

On 1 January 1947, the colliery passed into NCB ownership and initially some locomotives from the Lilleshall Company fleet were transferred with

the mine to operate the colliery and move the coal trains down to the interchange yard at Donnington. The locomotives transferred from Lilleshall ownership included one of the ex-Taff Vale/ex-GWR 0-6-2 tanks, *No.3* in unlined green, but the locomotive seems to have been little used, probably as the Lilleshall Company gave the NCB the loco they could most easily do without!

The Lilleshall Company then supplied one of its own-build (of 1869!) 0-6-0STs, no.6, in 1950, this locomotive was in unlined black, but the engine did not work for long, being scrapped in 1955. Given that the 0-6-0 Austerity tanks were considerably younger and more powerful it was a wonder that it lasted so long, getting to its eighty-sixth year.

Granville prospered in the post-war years, with production often around 300,000–350,000 tons per annum. It reached a peak of around 600,000 tons in the 1960s, when a new manager went for peak production. The mine was severely faulted, which almost led to its closure in 1972, but it was given a last-minute reprieve due to the energy crisis caused by the Arab–Israeli war of 1972–3. There was an underground shaft to assist in developing faces in seams affected by significant faults, for example

The NCB had delivered new to Granville Colliery an Andrew Barclay 0-4-0 and the locomotive remained at Granville until scrapped in late 1967. The locomotive never received a running number. *KIDDERMINSTER RAILWAY MUSEUM*

When the NCB acquired Granville Colliery in 1947, one of the ex-Granville locomotives sent to the NCB was ex-Taff Vale/ex-GWR 0-6-2 tank, No.35, which continued to work at Granville until 1954. *K.J. COOPER COLLECTION IRS*

A general view of the yards at Granville Colliery and of the locomotive sheds sometime in the late 1960s. *D. CLARKE*

Granville no.5 *newly delivered in 1952 to the colliery. The locomotive was subsequently fitted with a Geisel ejector to improve coal consumption. The locomotive continued to work at the colliery until April 1970.* D. CLARKE

Granville Colliery had a two-road locomotive shed built by the NCB in the 1950s that was capable of holding four locomotives. Here, two of the Austerity 0-6-0 tanks can be seen, with Granville no.5 *on the left fitted with a Geisel ejector and* No.8 *on the right.* D. CLARKE

Abbey Wood and Great East. One of the shafts was deepened from the 1,227ft (374m) reached in 1860 to 1,332ft (406m) in the 1950s, penetrating the carboniferous limestone and becoming the deepest shaft in the coalfield. Following the closure of Kemberton Mine in 1967, men transferred to Granville and almost 900 men were being employed. This number quickly fell to about 600 men in the 1970s.

The NCB added to the locomotive fleet with the purchase of Austerity 0-6-0 tank engines. The first arrived in August 1947, still in War Department livery and unnumbered (this was Hunslet-build no.2895 of 1943), but carrying WD no.75046. This engine later received an all-blue livery, but without lining. Subsequently, further Austerity 0-6-0 tank locomotives were purchased, with nos 3, 8 and 5; the latter was given the name *Granville no.5.* Subsequently, the ex-WD unnumbered locomotive and *Granville no.5* were fitted with Geisel oblong ejectors, which meant they had very distinctive chimneys. In July 1969, the livery of *Granville no.5* was black with red coupling rods, a smoke box painted red oxide and a red background to the nameplate.

In addition to the Austerity 0-6-0 tanks, Granville had a number of other steam locomotives including *Holly Bank no.3*, which arrived in June 1966 and was painted blue with red coupling rods, red axle ends and red-backed nameplates. The locomotive only lasted a few years and was scrapped in July 1968. *The Colonel*, a 0-6-0 saddle tank, arrived in October 1963 and was painted royal blue lined in pale blue with red-backed nameplates. The locomotive was scrapped in 1966.

The larger locomotives worked the trains down to the exchange sidings at Donnington, but there were also lighter duties at the slag-crushing plant and the disposal site at the Rookery, as well as shunting the upper yards and colliery screens. The colliery had a Barclay 0-4-0 saddle tank that was delivered new in 1948 and, like other Granville locomotives, did not carry a running number, just NCB West Midlands Division on the black tank sides. This locomotive was too small for the trains down to Donnington and back, but was popular

Close-up of the nameplate for Granville no.5 *delivered new to* Granville Colliery on 10 May 1952. D. CLARKE

on the upper yard and colliery screens and the Landsale Yard. It was scrapped on site between August 1967 and March 1968.

In 1969, two Hunslet 0-6-0 diesels (nos 1D and 2D) were delivered brand new and replaced the last steam locomotives. This fleet was subsequently beefed up with the addition of a similar Hunslet from West Cannock Colliery (no.6D). The three diesels were painted in an unlined royal blue livery. The colliery closed in May 1979 and the last train ran down to the exchange sidings on 2 October 1979. Following closure, the three shunters were transferred away, with 2D being scrapped in 1985, but 6D was preserved by the Steamtown Railway Museum in Carnforth.

In June 1966, Holly Bank no.3 moved to Granville Colliery and remained until July 1968. Unusually for a Granville locomotive it was painted a bright blue with red-backed nameplates. The photo is at Holly Bank Colliery before the engine moved from there to Granville. D. CLARKE

In the 1960s, a number of engines were sent to Granville Colliery, including The Colonel, *a Hudswell Clarke 0-6-0 saddle tank, which arrived in October 1963 after an overhaul and was painted in royal blue. The engine was withdrawn in October 1966. D. CLARKE*

Granville Colliery continued to supply coal to Buildwas Power Station until closure in 1979. In the 1970s, the wagons used changed from the BR 16-ton unbraked mineral wagons to the new air-braked hopper wagons seen here. The brake van on the left dates from the early 1920s and was only used on internal traffic.

The arrival of the diesels in 1969 overlapped the use of steam locomotives, as two of the Austerity tanks were kept as spares, not being scrapped until 1970 (*Granville no.5* and the ex-WD engine) with one of them, no.8, being moved away to work at West Cannock Colliery and subsequently Bickershaw Colliery. It is now preserved on the East Lancashire Railway.

Granville Colliery shed and yard in the snow in the 1960s. Two Austerity 0-6-0 STs are visible, with the internal use only wagons on the right. These wagons would be used for moving coal to the land sale yard or for removing spoil from the pit, but would not be allowed to run on the BR network.
D. CLARKE

CHAPTER 9

Locomotive Depots

Wellington

The visual appearance of the locomotive shed at Wellington gave away its origins as a two-road goods shed. Up to 1867, the GWR locomotives had been stabled at nearby Ketley, but with the building of the line to Market Drayton there was a greater need for the servicing and stabling of locomotives, so in 1867 a proposal was made to convert the goods shed into a three-road locomotive depot, which was completed shortly afterwards.

The depot provided locomotives for the GWR branches to Much Wenlock and to Crewe, as well as locomotives for shunting at the Wellington goods yards and also local freight services. The depot had freight workings to Shrewsbury and Oxley (Wolverhampton), as well as some passenger workings to and from Wolverhampton. After Nationalization, the depot also provided locomotives for the interchange sidings at Trench (following the closure of the ex-LNWR shed in 1943) and trip workings to and from the Central Ordnance Depot at Donnington. The original coaling stage was replaced in the mid-1950s and the small 42ft (13m) turntable was removed in 1950.

For most of its life as a depot, Wellington shed always had a sizeable allocation of pannier tanks. Here, in May 1957, nos 3760 and 5712 can be seen along with other unidentified members of the class. The origins of the shed as a goods shed before conversion to an engine shed can be clearly seen. D. CLARKE

For the services from Wellington to Crewe and return, Wellington shed in the 1930s had a motley collection of elderly GW engines. Here, no.3201, a Stella Class 2-4-0, is seen light-engine in the station. B. POTTER

The depot's principal locomotives were tank engines, although in the 1930s the depot had some elderly GWR Duke, Bulldog 4-4-0s, Stella and Barnum Class 2-4-0s for working the passenger trains to Crewe. The last Barnum 2-4-0s, nos 3210 and 3222, were withdrawn from Wellington in early 1937. The two Bulldog 4-4-0s, nos 3358 *Tremayne* and 3445 *Flamingo*, continued on the Crewe trains until late 1945, when they were also withdrawn.

In BR days, the principal passenger engines were some ex-GWR 2-6-2 tanks of 41XX and 51XX varieties, which had replaced the 44XX 2-6-2 tanks that left Wellington in 1951. Revisions to the line and platforms allowed the larger and more powerful tanks to replace the 44XX locomotives on the Much Wenlock trains, with the rest of the allocation being 0-6-0 pannier tanks of various classes. The closure of Trench shed in 1943 brought an ex-Caledonian 0-4-0 saddle tank to the shed and ex-LNWR loco-

motives from the Coalport branch would also be seen there. In December 1938, the shed's work was scheduled as shown in the table.

One of Wellington's locomotives, Bulldog 4-4-0 no.3437, was also out stationed at Crewe Gresty Lane for the Wellington services.

The shed's coaling facilities were a little primitive, with the coaling being done by a bucket and a manual winch that required two people to operate. Relief was at hand, however, when in 1949 the manual winch was replaced by an electric hoist. However, when the decrepit coaling shed was demolished, a small crane with electric-operated bucket was used. A new coaling shelter in asbestos was built in the late 1950s and an electric hoist used again.

The front of the shed clad in timber seems to have disappeared in stages in the late 1930s and was never replaced, leading to a somewhat ramshackle appearance.

Wellington Shed's Workings, December 1938

Class	Turns	Engines
Bulldog 4-4-0	I passenger	3445 *Flamingo*
Earl 4-4-0	I passenger	3208
51XX 2-6-2 tank	I passenger, I goods	5142, 5165, 5177, 5195
44XX 2-6-2 tank	2 passenger, I goods	4401, 4409
57XX 0-6-0PT	I passenger	3775, 9748
645 0-6-0PT	2 goods, I shunting shared with the 1854 and 850 classes	1808
1854 0-6-0PT		1762, 1762
850 0-6-0PT		1917, 1949

The 44XX 2-6-2 tanks were allocated to Wellington from 1934 to 1951, when they were transferred away, except 4400, which was withdrawn from Wellington in April 1951. Here, 4400 is on-shed at Wellington on 13 November 1948. D. CLARKE

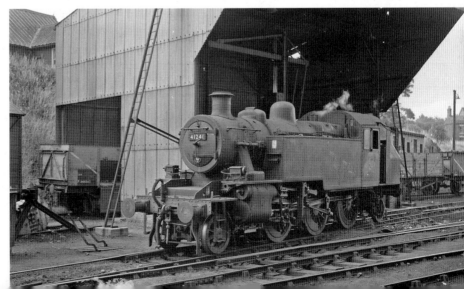

For the Crewe trains, Wellington shed used ex-GWR 2-6-2 tanks, pannier tanks, or the ex-LMS 2-6-2 tanks. Here, no.41241 sits on Wellington shed. The loco survived the closure of the shed, moving to Skipton in Yorkshire, and was subsequently preserved on the Keighley and Worth Valley Railway. COLOUR RAIL

The original coal stage for Wellington shed had become almost derelict and was replaced in the late 1950s, but is here shown in the state that it had become before being demolished. R. CARPENTER

From 1958 to 1960, Wellington had a small allocation of the BR Standard Class 3 tanks. Here, no.82006 is seen on-shed awaiting its next duty, having arrived from Newton Abbot shed in September 1959. D. CLARKE

For a number of years, ex-LMS 0-4-4 tank no.41900 could be seen stored adjacent to the coaling stage in the locomotive depot. It had arrived in August 1960 for the Wenlock branch, but does not appear to have been used. It was withdrawn in March 1962 and sent for scrap. HMRS

For a short time in May 1960, ex-LMS Stanier 2-6-4 tank no.42645 was allocated for a regular goods train to and from Wellington to Oxley. An unusual allocation to the depot occurred in August 1960, when no.41900, an ex-LMS 0-4-4 tank, was tried on the Much Wenlock trains, but was quickly dispatched to storage and remained unused at the depot until sent away for scrap in March 1962.

The depot was also used occasionally for winter storage of locomotives from the Cambrian lines, so, for example, Dukedog 4-4-0s nos 9004, 9014 and 9018 arrived for storage in September 1959, before being steamed in April 1960 to return to their home depot of Wrexham (Croes Newydd).

The depot's location on the main line also meant that locomotives being moved to and from works could be seen temporarily on the depot and, as an example, outside-cylinder pannier tanks nos

1501/2/9 were seen at the depot before being taken to a private works for overhaul, as the engines had been sold to the NCB. It was also not unusual to see locomotives not allocated to the depot on-shed, having worked in trains to Wellington or to Hollinswood. One of Shrewsbury's Jubilees was also seen on-shed in the early 1960s.

In 1959, there were ninety-two staff based at the depot, with thirty-two drivers, thirty-two firemen, as well as fitters, boiler smiths and clerical staff.

The location of the shed on the GWR main line meant that it was a convenient location for locomotives being towed to main works for attention, particularly as Wellington was close to Wolverhampton Stafford Road works. Locomotives had to be towed at slow speed and so as not to block the main line they would journey in stages to get to their destination.

For a period in the late 1950s, Wellington shed was used for the winter storage of engines from the Cambrian line depots. Here, Dukedog no.9014 is stored at the rear of the shed. With the increase in traffic in the spring, the loco would be steamed and returned back to its parent depot, in this case Croes Newydd. D. CLARKE

Nos 4158 and 42645 are seen on-shed at Wellington in 1960. 4158 was a Wellington engine for many years, but 42645 was unusual, having been briefly allocated to Wellington from May 1960 specifically for a Class E freight from Wellington to Wolverhampton Oxley.
RAIL ONLINE

Wellington shed was often used as a staging post for locomotives being towed for main works attention. Here, 7922 Salford Hall of Shrewsbury is probably on its way to Wolverhampton works on 18 January 1959. The cloth on the chimney signifies that it has been stored.
D. CLARKE

A unusual resident at Wellington shed was no.92, which had been built in 1857 by Beyer Peacock as a 0-4-2 saddle tank, but was rebuilt in 1878 as a 0-4-0 tank. It was used to provide hot water for boiler washing-out from 1939 to 1946. LENS OF SUTTON

The ex-GWR locomotives still allocated to the shed in the early 1960s were given the standard BR overhead electric warning flashes not usually applied to Western Region locomotives, but with most of Wellington's allocation working into Crewe it became a necessity.

The depot in BR days was part of the Western Region and had a shed code of 84H, but with Regional boundary changes it became part of the London Midland Region in September 1963. It was renumbered 2M, but on 10 August 1964 it was closed. The last locomotives on-shed on closure day were nos 3744, 3776, 9630, 9639 and 9774. All of these locomotives were transferred away for further duty, the author seeing 9630 and 9639 at Croes Newydd shed the following year. The shed was then demolished and the site is now a car park.

Before the depot closed to steam, 08 shunter no.D3028, without yellow warning stripes, was seen on-shed, but it is not known to the author why it was there. With the closing of the depot, a 08 0-6-0 diesel shunter was allocated to the goods yard in the 1970s and no.08 3397 was seen on a train from Madeley Junction with a load from the Horsehay Company in 1971. Another of the class, no.08 590, was observed at Wellington bringing a train from the Ordnance Depot in Donnington to the yard at Wellington in June 1976.

Trench Sidings

Very little is known of the origins of this shed, but it opened around 1870 and the single-road building was of wooden construction with a corrugated iron roof. The shed was adjacent to the Shropshire Union main line and was built to serve an industrial complex nearby, which was adjacent to the canal basin at the foot of the Trench Inclined Plane. The sidings curved away at 90 degrees from the main line and the curvature of the track and the tight curves within the works necessitated the use of short-wheelbase tank engines.

The sidings serviced Trench Ironworks and Shropshire Ironworks (both companies under the same ownership from 1872), which manufactured steel wire and rod. The engine from Trench Sidings also served the Wombridge branch, which opened in 1866, but the branch was truncated in 1873. When the Shropshire Union was taken over by the LNWR, its Shrewsbury depot became responsible for supplying a locomotive for the duties at Trench, usually an ex-LNWR Webb 0-4-0 saddle tank.

The *LNWR Working Time Table* of 1909 stated that the shunting locomotive at Trench Sidings would be in operation from 8.30am until 7.30pm and on Saturdays would work from 8.30 am until 4.00pm.

Following the absorption of the LNWR by the LMS, the usual locomotive was an ex-Caledonian Railway 0-4-0 saddle tank, with nos 16004 and 16027 being noted during the 1930s. When the ex-CR railway locos were not available, an ex-Lancashire and Yorkshire (L&Y) 0-4-0 saddle tank, no.11218, was used, for example in September 1938. In 1925 (soon after the creation of the LMS), the shed had five staff allocated to the depot for duties that also included shunting down the line at Donnington. However, as traffic reduced, so did the number of men at the depot, reaching a point where only two men worked from the shed. A special shunt wagon built by the LNWR was based at Hadley Junction and also used at Trench Sidings.

The shed was closed in 1943 as the volume of shunting had reduced and did not justify out-stationing an engine at Trench. The two sets of loco crews were transferred to Wellington along with

The usual shunter based at Trench was an ex-Caledonian 0-4-0 and no.16004 is seen in the late 1930s. The siding where the photographer was standing belonged to the Lilleshall Company and was used for offloading coal out of wagons into coal merchants' lorries, hence the pile of coal. D. CLARKE

the locomotive (at this time Caledonian 0-4-0 tank no.16027), but remained under the control of Shrewsbury LMS shed. On a daily basis the loco would work the LMS yard in Wellington (the loco crew booking on at 5.00am) until 10.15am, before setting off light-engine to Hadley Junction and then to a number of private sidings at Hadley, Trench and Donnington (but not the Ordnance Depot). As the locomotive would require a second crew part way through the day, they would catch the bus to Hadley, with the first crew booking off at 1.00pm. The locomotive would then work a trip from Hadley to Donnington and another trip from Donnington back to Hadley, then work light-engine back to Wellington, the crew booking off at 7.30pm.

If the ex-Caledonian 0-4-0 was not available, an ex-L&Y 0-4-0 pug was used, or on occasions one of Shrewsbury's elderly Webb 0-6-0 coal engines; this was the last engine to use the turntable before it was removed in 1950. The Caledonian 0-4-0 tank remained at Wellington until October 1950, when one of Wellington's ex-GWR pannier tanks was provided to shunt the sidings on an as-required basis. The 0-6-0 pannier tanks could be used on the duties as the locomotives were no longer required to shunt the tight curves within the ironworks, as the private sidings agreement had been terminated in 1946. Shunting the sidings adjacent to the works in later years was complicated by the fact that the ex-GWR pannier tanks were too heavy to cross a weighbridge just over the road level crossing, so wagons had to be propelled into the works at speed. The pannier tanks were also prohibited from using the Back Road due to the sharp curvature and poor condition of the track. The company operating the works at this time was Summerfield's, a fabrication company, and it provided a tractor to move wagons around the works. The interchange sidings were simplified, but as some traffic still used the line into the works, trackwork remained although overgrown with weeds. The line servicing Summerfield's closed in April 1968.

Despite the shed being closed in 1943 it was still standing in the mid-1960s, but was subsequently demolished. Today, the site is unrecognizable as the creation of the Trench interchange road lowered the ground level and totally transformed the site.

Coalport

When the LNWR branch from Wellington was opened on 10 July 1861, a two-road engine shed was opened at Coalport. The engines were supplied from the LNWR depot at Shrewsbury and at one point seven engines were stabled at the shed for both passenger and freight traffic.

As passenger trains when the line first opened were hauled by Webb 0-6-0 saddle tanks, they would have been allocated to the shed, but these engines were soon replaced on the passenger trains by Webb 2-4-2 tanks. The passenger trains terminated at Wellington, which was a Great Western depot, but arrangements were made for the LNWR engines to be serviced at the depot if required. However, by the 1920s the allocation was down to one passenger engine and one freight locomotive. In 1925, ten men were based at the depot with two engines allocated, but by the early 1950s the shed was staffed by two sets of men for passenger work and one set for freight.

During the LNWR and LMS period, the locomotives allocated and serviced at the depot were LNWR Webb 2-4-2 tanks, 0-6-2 coal tanks and 0-6-0 tender engines; these consisted of coal engines, 0-6-0 DX goods or 0-6-0 'cauliflowers'. During the LMS era, ex-LNWR 0-8-0s were regularly seen working on the branch.

During the 1920s, the shed suffered from subsidence, such that the second road in the shed was removed to allow for the reinforcing of one of the shed walls.

After Nationalization, the shed was transferred to the Western Region so Wellington was responsible for providing staff. However, for a few years afterwards Shrewsbury was still responsible for providing locomotives, so ex-LMS locomotives predominated. Ex-LNWR 0-6-2 coal tanks nos 7746 and 7755 were seen in 1947, while 27609 and 27664 were seen in 1950. No.48904 was seen working passenger trains along with no.58926. This last locomotive had a charmed life, as it had been withdrawn just before the outbreak of World War II in 1939, but was reinstated and overhauled. After withdrawal in 1959, it was rescued and preserved and can be seen on the Keighley and Worth Valley Railway in Yorkshire.

Ex-LNWR 2-4-2 tanks were still in service in 1947, with 6757 seen on the line. After the demise of the elderly ex-LNWR engines, Shrewsbury supplied some Fowler Class 2 2-6-2 tanks. These were used on passenger services until they ceased in May 1952. The locos were nos 40005, 40008, 40048 and 40058.

For the last few years of operation, two sets of men were assigned for the passenger workings and one set for freight. During the 1950s, the freight workings were handled by Wellington's

pannier tanks and ex-LNWR G2 0-8-0s, as well as ex-Midland 3F 0-6-0s from Shrewsbury. The shed remained derelict for many years until demolition in the 1960s.

Ordnance Depot, Donnington

To service the sidings and the extensive warehouses, a small locomotive depot was built adjacent to the main line. It was initially stocked with steam locomotives, mainly Austerity 0-6-0s, which remained in use until 1962. From 1943, it is reported that two of the USA-built 0-6-0 tank engines were used before being sent to Europe from the middle of 1943. The Austerity tanks were replaced with Ruston diesel shunters starting in 1961 and these diesel shunters remained until 1991, when the COD Depot ceased to use rail traffic.

An ex-LNWR 0-6-0 Coal engine, no. 8148 stands alongside the carriage sheds at Coalport (LNWR) station in the 1930s. R. CARPENTER

APPENDIX

The Allocation of Locomotives to the Depots in the Telford Area

Coalport (LNWR)

A sub-shed of Shrewsbury, in the early 1900s up to seven engines were allocated to the depot. However with falling traffic in 1925, two engines were allocated with ten staff at the depot. As Shrewsbury supplied the locomotives the individual engines allocated to Shrewsbury could be seen at Coalport. Regular engines included:

Coal Tank 0-6-2 tanks: in LMS days, 7742,7746, 7755, 27609 and 27664; in BR days, 58904 and 58926

Fowler 2-6-2 tanks, from 1947: 40005, 40008, 40058

In the event of the non-availability of any locomotive, Shrewsbury would arrange for a substitute to be provided. With the closure of the passenger service in June 1952 the shed closed and the remaining drivers and firemen transferred to Wellington. Freight requirements were then provided principally by Wellington.

Much Wenlock (GWR)

This was a sub-shed of Wellington with engines out-stationed from Wellington, and shared the passenger and freight services to Wellington and Craven Arms with Wellington's locomotives. The shed was a single-road affair with room for two tank engines under cover. The shed closed in December 1951 and the drivers and firemen were transferred to Wellington. Wellington then supplied the motive power for the line.

The following locomotives were known to have been out-stationed at Much Wenlock:

1902:	645 Class 0-6-0 saddle tanks nos 1502, and 1802
1905:	645 Class 0-6-0 tanks nos 1541, 1790 and 1801
1913:	517 Class 0-4-2 Tanks nos 521 and 1479
1921:	517 Class 0-4-2 tank no.521. 645 Class 0-6-0 no.1531
1934:	655 Class 0-6-0 tank no.1779 5800 Class 0-4-2 tank 5811

In the 1930s the allocation of the 44XX 2-6-2 tanks was shared between Wellington and Much Wenlock, with nos 4400, 4401, 4403, 4406 and 4409 working the line until Wenlock shed closed, the engines being transferred away

Trench Sidings

With only one engine allocated, this shed was a sub-shed of Shrewsbury. In LNWR days a Webb 0-4-0 Tank was allocated but no confirmation of a number. In LMS days ex-Caledonian 0-4-0 Saddle Tanks nos 16004 and 16027 were allocated at different times. When the ex-Caledonian 0-4-0 was not available an ex-L&Y 0-4-0 saddle Tank, 11218, was seen on shed. Five staff were at the shed.

MoD Donnington

With the opening of the Depot in the 1940s, the depot had an extensive allocation for an industrial site and included the following:

- USA 0-6-0 tanks nos 1426 and 1952 from 1943, but how long they remained is not known. These locomotives were built in America and intended to replace damaged locomotives once the allies had invaded Europe, but before the invasion in 1944 they were put to use in the UK.
- Austerity, 0-6-0 Saddle tanks. Between 1943 and 1945 the following locos were allocated (but not all at the same time): nos 75019, 5065, 75068, 75157, 75161, 5093, 71487 and 5117. With the Second World War ending, the allocation of this class to Donnington was dynamic with a total of fourteen different engines being allocated at various times. From 1957 until the early 1960s the following were based at Donnington with three locomotives being able to handle the traffic: nos 138, 104 and 187.

From 1961 a small number of Ruston and Hornsby 0-6-0 Diesel Hydraulic shunters replaced the Austerity steam locomotives, the first three arriving being nos 429, 430 and 431. From the 1970s other locomotives of this class were also seen including 434, 427, 420, 432 and 433.

In the 1970s a couple of 0-4-0 diesels were also allocated to the depot: one built by Vulcan Foundry, 224, and one built by North British, 405.

In the 1980s the big 0-6-0 diesel hydraulics were supplemented by three four-wheeled diesel hydraulics built by Thomas Hill, nos 253, 254 and 256.

The army had an extensive fleet of locomotives to service the large number of sites it managed and there was constant movement of engines from one site to another. It is also not clear if all the locomotives listed above actually worked at the depot as some may have been allocated there for storage before moving on. This particularly applies during the Second World War.

Locomotives Allocated to Wellington Shed

1914
'323' Class 2-4-0
3234
3240

1921

645 Class 0-6-0 Tank	'Barnum' Class 2-4-0
759	322
1510	
1554	

'655' Class 0-6-0 Tank	'221' Class 0-6-0
1748	2076 (1901)
1778	2108 (1906)
1787	2061 (1954)
2710	

'517' Class 0-4-2 Tank	'645' 0-6-0 PT (1930s)
842	1523
1424	
1485	

'850' Class 0-6-0 Tank

1920–30s
Complete allocations for the 1920–30s have not been found but the following locomotives were known to have been at Wellington. Where known the period has been indicated.

Stella Class 2-4-0		Barnum Class 2-4-0	
3201	(1931)	3210	(–1937)
3204	(1922–9)	3221	(–1933)
3205	(1929)	322	(–1937)
3518	(1931–3)	323	(–1936)

Duke Class 4-4-0		Bulldog Class
3266	*Amyas* (1930s)	3309 *Mariston* (withdrawn 1934)
		3405 *Empire of India* (withdrawn 1937)
		3414 *Sir Edward Elgar* (withdrawn 1937)
		3445 *Flamingo* (to Stafford Road 1938)

1947

Bulldog Class 4-4-0	44XX 2-6-2 Tank
3417	4400

53XX Class 2-6-0	4403
5309	4406
5332	5127
	5135

'221' Class 0-6-0	5137
230	5178

57XX 0-6-0 Pannier Tank
3732
3775
5758
9624
9630
9639

1950s to closure in 1964

1600 Class 0-6-0 PT
1663   (1957–8)

5700 Class 0-6-0 PT

3626	(1959–62)	7754	(1957–9)
3532	(1957–62)	9621	(1959–61)
3744	(1957–64)	9630	(1957–64)
3749	(1957–8)	9636	(1960–3)
3760	(1957–8)	9639	(1957–64)
3776	(1962–64)	9741	(1957–62)
4605	(1959–62)	9742	(1957)
5712	(1957)	9774	(1957–64)
5758	(1957–8)		

1950s to closure in 1964 (contd)

5100 Class 2-6-2 T		6400 Class 0-6-0 PT	
4110	(1957–9)	6421	(1961–2)
4120	(1957–62)	6429	(1961–2)
4142	(1957–8)		
4154	(1960s)		
4158	(1957–62)		
4178	(1960–2)		

Ex-LMS Class 2 2-6-2 T
41201 (1959–64)
41204 (1960–63)
41231 (1960–61)
41232 (1960–64)
41241 (1959–64)

Ex-LMS 2P 0-4-4T	BR Class 3 2-6-2T	
41900 (1961–2)	82004	(1959–60)
	82006	(1959–60)
	82007	(1958)
	82009	(1958)
	82030	(1959–60)
	82038	(1959–60)

Further Reading and Bibliography

Gale, W.V. and Nicholls, C.R., *The Lilleshall Company Ltd: A History 1764–1964* (Moreland Publishing). A book long out of print, detailing the history of the Lilleshall Company.

Jones, Ken, *The Wenlock Branch. Wellington to Craven Arms* (Oakwood Press, 1998). An excellent (now out of print) book, but worth tracking down. The author had a unique insight into the area and the line to Much Wenlock, as he was in his youth a fireman and later a driver at Wellington shed and was born at Lightmoor in the heart of the Coalbrookdale coalfield. The book also considers the people who made the railway work and their stories. In the author's view, one of the best histories of a branch line ever published.

LNWR Marshalling Circular July, August, September 1910. This details the through coaches used by the LNWR and the make-up of express trains and postal trains.

LNWR Working Time Tables of Shropshire, February 1909.

Mitchell, Vic and Smith, Keith, *Stafford to Wellington* (Middleton Press, 2014).

Trinder, Barrie, *The Industrial Archaeology of Shropshire*, Third Edition, 2000 (Phillimore and Company, ISBN 1 86077 133 5. A very readable history of the area by an eminent historian.

Yate, Bob, *The Railways and Locomotives of the Lilleshall Company* (Irwell Press, 2008). The Lilleshall Company has not been well covered by the railway press, but this book does an excellent job of detailing the history of the company and its use of the railways.

Yate, Bob, *The Shropshire Union Railway. Stafford to Shrewsbury Including the Coalport Branch* (Oakwood Press, 2003).

The author has also used the reprints of the 1901 Ordnance Survey plans republished by Alan Godfrey, there being fourteen maps covering the Telford area. Looking at these maps clearly shows the number of abandoned mines, ironworks and brick- and tileworks that covered the area. The reverse of each map gives details from *Kelly's Directory* and also has notes from Barrie Trinder, a leading authority on the Industrial Revolution in Shropshire. Thoroughly recommended.

The following magazine articles were also referenced:

Bradshaw, David and Jenkins, Stanley, 'Three Rails Around Oakengates', *Steam Days*, March 2001.

Cowgill, H.A., 'Pre-War Goods work at Ketley', *Great Western Railway Journal*, no.14, Spring 1995.

Groves, Matty, 'Wellington Shed', *British Railways Illustrated*, Volume 10, April 2001.

Jenkins, Stanley, 'The Wellington to Craven Arms Line', *Steam Days*, February 2003.

Page, Michael, 'Commuting to Wellington', *Steam Days*, April 1997.

Smith, Martin, 'Coal, Iron and the Wenlock Edge', *British Railways Illustrated*, August 1996.

Smith, William and Turner, Chris, 'Wellington', *Great Western Journal*, no.33 Spring 2000.

Smith, William H., 'The Coalport Branch', *British Railway Journal*, no.19, 1987.

Wilson, Bryan I., 'Premier Line to Coalport', *Railway Bylines*, April 1999.

One of the few remaining artefacts of the Lilleshall Company is the bridge girders in Oakengates, proudly showing the company name. G. CRYER

Index

RELATED TITLES FROM CROWOOD

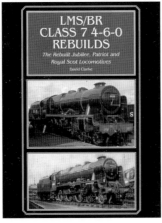

LMS/BR Class 7 4-6-0 Rebuilds
DAVID CLARKE
ISBN 978 1 84797 651 2
208pp, 240 illustrations

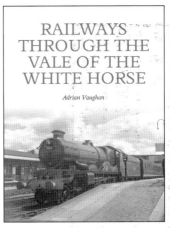

Railways Through the Vale of the White Horse
ADRIAN VAUGHAN
ISBN 978 1 84797 871 4
160pp, 240 illustrations

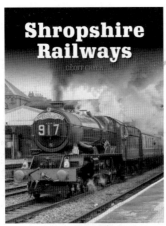

Shropshire Railways
GEOFF CRYER
ISBN 978 1 84797 691 8
160pp, 200 illustrations

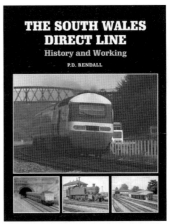

The South Wales Direct Line
P.D. RENDALL
ISBN 978 1 84797 707 6
208pp, 160 illustrations

In case of difficulty ordering, please contact the Sales Office:

The Crowood Press
Ramsbury
Wiltshire
SN8 2HR
UK

Tel: 44 (0) 1672 520320

enquiries@crowood.com

www.crowood.com